EXPLORERS, DREAMERS AND THIEVES

Writers in the Archives of the British Museum

First published by Charco Press 2024
Charco Press Ltd., Office 59, 44-46 Morningside Road,
Edinburgh EH10 4BF

ISBN: 9781913867942
e-book: 9781913867959

www.charcopress.com

Coordinated by Carolina Orloff
Edited by Fionn Petch & Fiona Mackintosh
Cover designed by Pablo Font
Typeset by Laura Jones-Rivera
Proofread by Fiona Mackintosh

EXPLORERS, DREAMERS AND THIEVES

Writers in the Archives of the British Museum

Selva Almada
Rita Indiana
Josefa Sánchez Contreras
Philippe Sands
Juan Gabriel Vásquez
Gabriela Wiener

Translated by
Anne McLean • Robin Myers • Carolina Orloff
Fionn Petch • Frances Riddle

CHARCO PRESS

Contents

PREFACE

AN ADVENTURE AMONG THE ARCHIVES

Writing is, by definition, an exploration. The author's vocation is to be adventurous and, as such, writing responds to a desire to immerse oneself in the past, in memory, in one's own existence and imagination. To begin to write a story is to embark on a journey towards the creation of a narrative. It is no coincidence that many of the great explorers have also been great writers. Hay Festival has always encouraged this relationship between creativity, adventure and reinterpretation of the world from different angles. Many of the participants in the various editions of the festival over the decades have shared on stage the narratives around the explorations that led them to tell stories.

This book takes a novel approach to creative writing based on the encounter between the complex histories of Europe and America. After the success of *Untold Microcosms* in 2022, the curatorial team at SDCELAR and the Hay Festival joined forces again to invite a group of authors to draw inspiration from objects housed at the museum. This time, the premise changed a little. On this occasion, the creators were invited to examine a series of ethnographic documents, or 'Eth docs': a vast collection of diaries, letters, sketches, reflections and transactions, all related to the process of acquisition at the museum. As such, these texts provide an explanation of how these objects arrived at the museum. The authors were invited to use these materials as a basis to create a narrative with the 'explorers, dreamers and thieves' who brought these works to the museum as inspiration. The process – described in detail in the introduction to this book – produced fascinating results. Unsurprisingly, the imagination of these authors takes us on extraordinary journeys.

Juan Gabriel Vásquez imagined a mind-bending journey through the Colombian jungle. Gabriela Wiener created an epistolary exchange between two brilliant poets. Philippe Sands followed the route of an arrowhead through several countries. Josefa Sánchez Contreras accompanied a group of Manche Ch'ol explorers. Selva Almada narrated the transformative dream of a migrant based on a conversation with his mother. Rita Indiana sang of Schomburgk's brick. Together, these stories form a narrative constellation full of possibilities. Indeed, the sum of these voices is an invitation to travel and to critical reflection. And they fulfil one of the premises of literature: to take readers to unknown places by means of language.

Explorers, Dreamers and Thieves is a volume where imagination and research meet. It is also, as was the case with its predecessor, an enriching and collaborative work that combines different perspectives and ways of understanding the past. The authors and readers of this book will continue this journey of imagination and reflection when they meet in the various Hay Festivals in Latin America and Europe. In the meantime, readers can engage with the multiplicity of voices presented here, following in the footsteps of the explorers, dreamers and thieves who inspired it.

Cristina Fuentes La Roche OBE
International Director, Hay Festival

Dr Laura Osorio Sunnucks
Santo Domingo Centre of Excellence for
Latin American Research, British Museum

Felipe Restrepo Pombo
Co-Editor of the Spanish edition

INTRODUCTION

The British Museum houses an eclectic assortment of undigitised paper files known as 'Ethnographic Documents' or 'Eth docs'. These archives range from early-nineteenth-century fragments of handwritten correspondence between curators, colonial officials and explorers to drawings, photographs, maps, newspaper cuttings and typewritten reports related to object acquisitions and archaeological excavations. This miscellaneous assemblage, haphazardly gathered and transcribed over time, has generally been considered secondary for museum research. For this project, we invited six authors to engage with these archives and use them as primary source material to create imagined and affectively charged narratives. The resulting anthology offers the public an opportunity to interact with these overlooked records and, by reconsidering the multiple perspectives they contain, it presents counter-narratives about Latin America and the Caribbean.

This is the second book in a project that expands the approach to writing about museum material, whether objects or archives. The first book, *Untold Microcosms*, invited authors to create fictions and personal reflections about objects in storage at the British Museum. By privileging evocative writing and individual perspectives, we sought to break with the impersonal and authoritative voice commonly used in museum texts. We hoped to highlight how the work happening in museums can be emotional; how the study of people and cultures can eschew the quest for objective truth or specialist knowledge, and how it can shape our sensibility towards the infinite ways in which we consider the world. We also aimed to mobilise speculation and creativity, displaying the potential of the imagination in understanding 'ethnographic' or world culture collections.

The first volume, which invited authors to explore the understudied object collections in storage, was successful beyond creating accessibility; the authors tackled the problematic lacunae in cultural representation, wove personal reveries into recorded collector biographies, and built futuristic contexts to imagine a less violent world. As curators who have mostly worked with makers or users, we found that the writings did not consistently deal with object materiality. We did not find this problematic; we agreed that it was partly because very few of the authors were able to visit the collection (the research for the project took place during the Covid-19 pandemic). Furthermore, we assumed that this tendency related to the preferred medium of the writers: words. So, for this second volume, we decided to encourage authors to work specifically with the 'Eth docs'. Perhaps unexpectedly for some, this material is not simply comprised of dry institutional descriptions; in many cases the documents contain a profusion of idiosyncratic expressions that perfectly evoke the personalities behind the exchanges.

The Material in Question

The heterogeneity and allusiveness of the 'Eth docs' makes them a compelling source for researchers, as well as a logistical challenge for librarians and archivists. The 'Eth docs' are currently stored in the basement of the British Museum's main site in Bloomsbury, held together by staples, paper clips or plastic folders, and organised in over two thousand envelopes stored on metal shelves. Although these archives initially included paperwork on collections from other parts of the world, given that they were created across the Museum's departments, today they remain separate from the central archives. Since 2004, they have existed as an annex of the Department of Africa, Oceania and the Americas (AOA) but their informal and scattered trajectory poses a challenge for any linear tracing of their origins. Early attempts to archive these documents date back to the beginning of the twentieth century, with progress made in the fifties and sixties, and an inventory created in the eighties. Although incomplete, this inventory assigned a number to each bundle of documents, grouped together by region, country, period, and/or collection. Sometimes, a brief description of the content of each envelope is provided. Most of the time, however, the subject matter is only revealed by opening the envelopes; by touching, looking, and reading.

The 'Eth docs' are public archives, which means that in theory anyone can request access to them. However, because they have not yet been comprehensively digitised and integrated with the Museum's online database, their very existence is not widely known. At present, the Museum is designing a new way of organising these documents. It aims to create 'object files': folders that are directly related to an object in the collection, that bring together these 'chaotic' documents, along with all the associated correspondence. This new archive will also be digitalised, facilitating partial public access to these unknown files. For now, though, the 'Eth docs' are one step further inside the Museum silo than the objects in storage.

In providing a range of direct and indirect information about the British Museum's object collections, the 'Eth docs' offer intimate insights into the interests, desires, fears and prejudices of individuals and institutions. By acknowledging the asymmetrical power relations behind the creation of historical archives and ethnographic museums intended to house impressive quantities of material for posterity, researchers and cultural practitioners have challenged the notion of the archive as a static and seemingly objective repository of evidence that produces knowledge as empirical truth. The fraught nature of the archive – what it contains, omits and distorts – and its relationship to coloniality, imperialism and Atlantic slavery have been the subject of sustained critique by scholars such as Michel-Rolph Trouillot[1] and Saidiya Hartman[2]. As a consequence of their work, the archive has emerged as a dynamic site with potential for multisensory encounters and transdisciplinary research. It is in the wake of these reflexive and experimental approaches that the six authors featured in this book have engaged with the Latin American and Caribbean 'Eth docs' at the British Museum.

---

1   See, for example, Michel-Rolph Trouillot (1995) *Silencing the Past: Power and the Production of History.*

2   Saidiya Hartman (2008) 'Venus in Two Acts', *Small Axe* 12 (2): 1-14.

Curating Eth docs

The tendency in museums to produce texts characterised by neutrality derives from their founding logics in the eighteenth-century European Enlightenment, wherein their core function was to build scientific knowledge for the good of society. As mentioned above, these logics have been troubled, at least theoretically, for decades, as researchers and practitioners have highlighted the systemically unjust apparatus that undergirds much anthropological work and many museums. Perhaps because of the seeming impossibility of fully disabling those core structures and creating meaningful reparations, the literature on museums is broadening discussions on how to restitute and repair historical violences to question institutional care: can museums ever really prioritise people – whether descendant communities, visitors, or even those working in the institution – over the collections they house?

The stories in this anthology are prefaced by collages, created by us, the curators of the materials used by the writers. These visual compositions mark our presence and reveal our involvement in the project, from its collaborative conceptual framing to the selection of images and documents we shared with the authors. As curators of the Latin America and Caribbean collections at the British Museum, our regular physical access to these 'Eth docs' provided us with the time and space to connect with the documents before sharing them with the writers. The iterative practice of unclipping and unfolding, reclipping and refolding these documents has allowed us to reflect on the haptic materiality of handling undigitised archives. In working with this kaleidoscope of marginal archival material related to Latin America and the Caribbean, an aesthetic of the fragment emerged.

We also consider our photomontage to represent the intimate connections between literature from the region and the archive; a relationship that itself can be seen to function as a mosaic. The authors in this anthology were invited to use imagination, personal position and emotion to evoke the people and relationships that have permeated the Museum over time. In turn, the 'visual page-breaks' and new stories invite you, the reader, to use similar approaches to re-read historical records; to chart new ways of re-positioning the past to envision radical futures.

Magdalena Araus Sieber,
Diego Atehortúa
and
Laura Osorio Sunnucks

A MEMORY OF THE WORLD

Selva Almada

A MEMORY OF THE WORLD

Selva Almada

Translated by Carolina Orloff

Since he started working in the hotel, just over a year ago, he's taken on different roles. Out of all of them, the one he enjoys the most is the one he's performing right now: he's currently in charge of the upkeep of the three pools. The family one, which is the biggest, the one for adults only, and the smallest of them of all, the pool with a bar, with a counter on one side, and stools and tall tables emerging from the water. It even has sun loungers covered in tiny blue tiles.

His shift starts at five in the morning, before dawn. It's still dark when he arrives but as soon as he starts moving, the first light of day follows suit, a brightness still tainted with night. The coppery rays of the first sun that begin to blend in with the lingering darkness. The last of the stars fall into that effervescent fire that puts them out like a cup over a candle.

The water is being filtered. He sees it turning in circles. The jets push from the sides and form whirlpools.

The sound from the pump is almost the only sound at that time of day, when all the guests are sleeping. The sound of the water brings with it sounds from his childhood, which feels distant to him although he's quite young, he hasn't hit thirty yet. He would be young if he was one of the many guys that come and stay at the hotel in groups of friends, and take over the pool with the bar, ordering drinks from the second they arrive round noon – after they've just woken up – and linger there, merry and tipsy, until 7 p.m. when it closes. Any guy is young before he turns thirty, but not him. Back in his village, transitioning from one stage of life into another is marked by very specific moments, when we cease being one thing to become something else, when we stop being a boy and start being a man. Just like up in the woods, like the life cycles of the woods, so it is with a person's life. A moment to change, to stop being one thing and start being something else. A specific moment in life experienced like a ceremony. You carry with you the memory of what you've lived through, of who you were before that present. Everything that you've experienced will remain in your future body's memory. Everything you've lived through will remain in the memory of the world even when you leave your body. He knows that. He learnt that perhaps even before he learnt to talk, to walk. Perhaps even before then, in his mother's womb, before coming out into this world and breathing air into his lungs for the first time.

So: water in his memories. The stream where he grew up, a branch of the Great River, inserting itself like a liquid root into the belly of the woods. When he was a kid, the woods were still woods and the stream was still a stream. He thought it was beautiful although the stories the old women insisted on telling clarified that it wasn't as beautiful as when they were kids, let alone as beautiful as what the old women used to say. He must admit, however, that when he left, as a young lad, the stream didn't resemble much the stream of his childhood. It had actually slimmed down, darkened.

In the pools of the hotel the water is so transparent that it hurts the eye. It burns in your nose, especially first thing in the morning, the smell of lye is so strong, when all the filter pumps are turned off and silence falls again on the park. The windows of hundreds of rooms, with their shutters closed, shut eyelids over the guests' dreams. It takes a while to become accustomed to all being quiet again. That's just one way of putting it, quiet. Once you clear your head from the noise of the pumps, you can hear a different kind of music. The birds in the woods – what's left of them – a narrow stretch between the built area and the road. Some of them are also found in the part of the wood he came from: great kiskadees, red-crested finches, thrushes. Others are completely new to him. He doesn't know what they're called but he's started to distinguish them by their song and their plumage. The one with the long feather in the tail, the small dotted one that hops along the ground, the one with the little crest, the one with the spiky beak. You can also hear the alligators, that soft froo froo sound they make with their tails as they drag themselves over the slabs, their claws scratching against the grass which is so short it's like a carpet. These alligators are also different to the ones he used to know: the overo alligators that he used to hunt with his brothers, with white tender flesh, so tender and bland that his mother had to season it well so that it had any taste at all. The yellow fat that the women keep to cure sprains and ease coughing fits. These ones here are called salamanders and have a crest on their head that runs all the way down their back, as if they had the spine in plain view. He likes seeing them move from the grass to the paving stones and back onto the grass. Turn bright green, then pale, back to green or brownish, depending on the grass.

His own reflection on the water, against the backdrop of small blue tiles, holding that long pole of the net he uses to collect all the tiny particles of rubbish the filter didn't catch, reminds him of the men in his village going fishing. He would see them from the shore. They would stand on their canoes, spear raised high in both hands, absolutely still, their eyes fixed on the water surface, waiting for a fish to swim past. They could stay still like that for hours and yet they could move so swiftly, so nimbly, launching the spear into the water and pulling it back out with their prey impaled, as quick as lightning. What were their thoughts while they waited? He used to observe them as a kid, and the only reason he wanted to be a man was to be able to stand on his own canoe, with his own spear, whittled and sharpened for days, and be ready. He wanted to be that man who comes back with a string of fish shining like the beads of a necklace.

His mobile vibrates in his trouser pocket. It's a WhatsApp message. He pulls it out and looks at it: an voice note from his mother. It's several minutes long. His mother sends voice notes as if she were dictating a letter.

Once the three pools are clean as mirrors, he puts his tools away and goes into the buffet kitchen to fetch a coffee. He walks past the maids who are mopping the floor. The yellow plastic signs warning of the wet floor are scattered all over the place. He greets his colleagues. He's familiar with some of them. They've shared beers in a bar downtown where they sometimes go after work. He knows their names. Some of them are new. Staff change frequently in the hotel. The company owns a chain of hotels all very similar to this one, so the personnel often get rotated. People also quit. They get tired and give up. They move and quit. He himself has quit other similar jobs before, many times. He has moved house many times.

Behind the kitchen there's a yard only for employees. Perhaps it's the only place apart from the toilets where guests can't see them. Here they can drink a cup of coffee, eat a sandwich or have a smoke. The coffee is black and quite strong. That's how he likes it. He'd never drunk coffee until he'd left his village. There the mornings begin with a sweet mate cocido. In winter, you would add a bit of milk, like children do before heading off to school. Afterwards the day would unfold in an endless succession of tereré. He listens to his mother's note with the phone close to his ear. He would be able to listen to it on loudspeaker without worrying about anyone understanding what she's saying, for his mother speaks to him in their own tongue, and no one understands it here. But he likes listening to her like this, as close to his ear as possible, his mother's voice entering his head as if the entire woods were also entering his head, the woods he hasn't visited in years, his mother aging in ways he cannot understand.

¡Chaco! Hey, Chaco! Chatting to the fancy lady?

Another colleague, one of the receptionists, has also got away to smoke and makes fun of him. He smiles and shrugs his shoulders without saying anything. When he pulls the phone away from his ear, the message cuts off. There's still half of it to go. He saves it for later.

When he arrived that morning his supervisor had said that once he was done with the pools, he has to replace the guy who looks for metal because he's called in sick. He knows how to use the metal detector, he's done it before many times. He likes it. Strolling up and down the shore, combing it with the detector. As he's doing this he sees the building of the new hotel is progressing fast. Soon this coast will be completely covered in concrete. It's hard for him to think that only three years ago, there was nothing at all. The low rainforest with its genuine palm trees, its miniature palms, its patches of succulents and its scrub, reached down to where just a very thin strip of beach began, so narrow it was like a line dividing the water from the jungle. He didn't get to see that. It must have been beautiful. When the new hotel is finished, there will no longer be any spaces on the beach free of people. There will be more work. More cans to fish for with the detector. More bodies turning red under the lashing sun. More waiters walking in their socks on the sand, carrying trays with cocktails in plastic cups. More rubbish. More seagulls eating rubbish.

After a shower, a beer and some food, he throws himself on the bed of the room he rents monthly. He turns off the light and plays the rest of his mother's message. When he reaches the end, he plays it again from the beginning, this time to listen to the entire message in one go. He doesn't reply because it's already late. But also because her voice notes, which are like letters, have the pace of letters, the pace of those conversations that don't require an immediate answer. A different sort of time, deliberately slower. He feels sleepy so he presses play on the message once more. He wants to go to sleep with his mother's voice in his ear, fall asleep holding her hand the way they'd enter the woods together when he was a kid...

I miss you, son. As you see, as you can hear, everything around here is so quiet that my own voice makes me jolt. You should see the state of things here, son. Or maybe best not to. Best that you don't see it. Best that you stay where you are and that I carry on missing you. Do you know? This is no place for a young man. Only the old folk remain here. And some women with young kids who cannot go to the city to work because they have no one to leave them with. We are here, of course, but we are old folk, old women and men that can hardly get by. D'you know? I dream a lot about the past. The dreams are getting longer and longer, and more detailed. Perhaps it's because lately I am sleeping more, although as you know us old women sleep less and less. We do so because soon enough we'll sleep for longer when we're dead. Old women like me never sleep very deeply but at the same time – and I find this odd – our dreams are very intense. Last night, for instance, I dreamt I was a bird, son. A gorgeous blue bird with very slender legs and a kind of boa of black feathers around the neck. I was a gorgeous blue bird flying above the woods. I could fly into the woods and through the trees. I was like a shuttle in a loom, stroking the tree branches with my beautiful blue feathers, and so I was weaving trees together, as if I were a bird and a spider at the same time. And suddenly, without knowing how – the way it always is in dreams, right son? – without knowing how I was no longer a bird. I was now a warrior. A young warrior that looked a bit like you, son. I was a warrior whose body looked like my son's or who was inside my son's body. And the feathers of the blue bird I had been until a few seconds before were now embroidered on the robe that, strangely enough, I had woven while flying, moving like a shuttle in a loom, from tree to tree. The robe covered me from head to ankles. It looked very similar to the clothes we used to wear for certain rituals when I was a little girl. You didn't get to see that, son. When you were born all of that was gone. I did see it with this very pair of eyes that see less by the day. But never mind. There is always less to be seen, don't you think? I think I've seen it all in my lifetime, and that what remains now is to look inward. And do you know what, son? You can look into yourself even if you cannot see. You don't need eyes for that. So back to the dream, I was a warrior who looked like you and I was dancing around fire. I was dancing more and more frantically, getting more and more out of control. Inside it felt like fire. I was dancing non-stop like a wild moth, wild like my robe embroidered with blue feathers. From outside the scene, if I took a few steps away from the bonfire and from the warrior that I was and who resembled you, from outside and at that distance away, I looked like a bird again. All of a sudden, from one second to the next, because of a spark or because of dancing so close to the flames, the robe caught fire. I woke up with the smell of burning feathers deep inside my nostrils. But you see, son, my dear lovely son, son that I miss so much, son, never forget that you must pay attention to your dreams. They don't come to you for no reason. Each morning I spend a little while thinking about the dream I had during that night. What did it come to tell me. What message did it bring for me from that place where dreams come from, which is not – believe me – very different to where the things we do, say, and think when awake come from. Sometimes we talk about this with my closest friend. We share our dreams while we clean water to drink. We have to talk more and more to find the plant that helps us clean the water. We have to leave it for longer and longer and stir more. Stir, stir, stir until your arms get tired of the movement and all of that effort so the water is barely drinkable. We clean it just enough so that you don't throw up your guts right after drinking it. Can you hear this silence, my son? You can't hear the wind. You can't hear the river. You can't hear the birds. I feel we are living in a desert, son. If you can hear the woods, like you say to me sometimes, it's because what you're hearing is the memory of the woods, the woods by heart, the woods that are inside you and that will go with you wherever you go. But here, right here from where I am talking to you, here, the place that knew how to be the heart of the woods, my son, today it's broken. The heart has stopped beating and the silence is horrifying.

That's why I like remembering the past, when you were not yet on this earth but you were already in me. I was only a little girl but of course you were already in me, waiting for me to grow up so that you could grow too. When I was a little girl and the plant to clean water was right there, easily found, when you didn't have to stir the plant in the water for so long, when it *seems that the herb was just an excuse, a way of perfuming the water, of giving it that flavour. The time when the stream was this full of fish and the woods this full of hares and mulitas and pigs. The time when my father's arms were not long enough to go all the way round one of the trees that used to be part of these woods. It would have been beautiful, son, for you to be next to me, for you to see the things I saw. And this is why I am telling you so that one day you can talk to your son about the things I saw. The memory of a world that no longer exists. Or better, a world that exists in me and in many other old men and women like me. It still exists, but not for long.*

A few weeks ago the pastors returned. You see them a lot less frequently now. Every now and then they come with bags of food and a tanker full of water. They bring the truck with water because we don't have any anywhere to store it. Often the truck returns to the city with its belly still full. The days when the pastors and the truck are here we fill ourselves up with water. You should see us, son, drinking that water as if it were alcohol. We get drunk on water, our bellies swollen with it. This is a desert but we don't act like desert animals yet. Even though we'd like to, our bodies are not prepared to hold water for when they cannot get it. I remember in the past, when I was a little girl, the pastors would come and go, they'd enter and leave the woods as if they were their home, bringing their god, the one and only... And we'd think: why bother having a single god when you can have so many? But still they convinced us. We stopped dancing to our song and began following theirs. And where is god now, that god that is one and only and almighty? The pastors took him away just as little by little they took our things, our homes, our woods. They've left us with nothing, those pastors, the Paraguayans. They even took god away with them, son, even god. That's why I like remembering the past, the stories that the grandmothers would tell, the stories where there were many gods and not just one. Sometimes the songs that I knew by heart when I was little also come back in my dreams.

The songs that the Paraguayans, the pastors, wanted us to forget while they taught us the psalms. But memories always remain somewhere, my son. There's no way around that. And those songs return to me, sometimes, in my dreams. I wake up singing them. And as the day unfolds, I forget them. They dry up like a puddle under the midday sun. D'you know what, son? Next time that I wake up singing one of them, I'll grab the phone and sing them to you, my little one, to see if you can remember them too, because you were already with me when I was a little girl, you were with me waiting for me to grow so that you could grow inside me too. So I reckon you will also remember them. Maybe one day we can sing them together. Not sure if around the same fire because, as I was saying, it's best if you don't come back. This is no place for young people, son.

The break of day is sad and it's raining. The rain is thin and relentless but he doesn't notice until he leaves the house and gets into his car. He drives in that rain, under that feeble curtain of water. He parks on the shoulder, about fifty metres from the hotel's main entrance; that's where the staff park. Second-hand cars, decrepit like his, all piled up in that improvised parking lot as if it were a scrap metal yard. He doesn't hurry to get out. It's early.

He winds the windows down and lights up a cigarette. From his shirt pocket, he pulls out a piece of paper folded in two. He unfolds it, puts the light on as it's still dark and looks at the drawing he made a few days ago. It's an axe. It's funny because when he heard his mother tell him about her dream (where she'd become a warrior that looked like him), he was still recalling a very vivid dream he'd had a few nights before. In it, he'd seen that axe he then drew as soon as he woke up. He was a young woman that looked a lot like his mother; like his mother was a long time before he was born. A still young girl who'd recently washed away her first bleeding in the stream. She and some other girls of her age (in the dream he was the girl) were digging up sweet potatoes from the edge of the wood, using the handle of an axe just like the one he would draw later. They worked and chatted; they were laughing out loud. He felt the laughter just below his waist, warming his pubis up. He was a gorgeous girl like his mother used to be. The friends in the dream were also beautiful. One hand was holding the axe while the other helped dig and bring up the sweet potatoes that grew in the blackened entrails of the soil. It was a pleasant dream, he enjoyed being in it, being a girl working away with her friends, chitchatting in whispers, laughing away. But suddenly a group of men came out of nowhere and attacked them. They defended themselves. He, the girl that she was and who looked a lot like his mother, buried the blade of the axe in the head of one of the men. He woke up gasping for air, his body covered in sweat. He was soaking as if he'd just emerged from one of the pools he cleans every morning. As if instead of being the pool cleaner he was one of the guests taking a quick plunge on a hot morning. All mornings were hot in that place. He grabbed a notepad and drew the axe. The memory was so clear he could feel the weight of the handle in his hand.

He folds the piece of paper in half again and puts it away in his pocket. Next time he has the day off, he will visit a tattoo parlour in town. He will ask the guy who works there to tattoo the axe on the palm of his hand.

He picks up the phone and holds it near his mouth. He starts speaking in his language.

Mamá, I had a dream. I was a beautiful young woman.

He falls quiet and deletes the message.

He starts again.

Hey, mamá. You know what? Last night I had a dream.

You and I were two beautiful young women digging up sweet potatoes at the edge of the woods.

He deletes the message again. He's scared of his own words, of narrating his dream out loud.

He steps out of the car and walks slowly towards the hotel entrance. It's still raining but he's going to get wet anyway as he cleans. In any case, the rain there never lasts very long.

The raindrops become tiny holes on the surface of the pool water. He stays still standing there on the edge, observing for a moment before switching on the pump. He remembers the last flood before he left his land. The rain lasting many days and many nights. The stream that started to swell until it burst its banks, the water overflowing in the streets of his village, entering the houses, rising up and up with every hour. The legs of the few pieces of furniture buried in the water. The pots and pans floating away. The dead animals floating away. People on the roofs. The help that never arrives or gets there too late. The water subsiding. That smell of rot that remains when the water dissipates.

Every time his mother sends him a message she tells him not to come back, that there is no place in the village for a young man. But nor is it a place for old people. What would his mother do if there was another flood like that one?

Before deciding to turn the pump on, he crouches down at the edge and swings a hand into the water. He wets his nose. Mixed with rain water, the smell of lye is diminished. A few salamanders have emerged from their caves. Stretched out on the paving stones, quiet as rocks, they raise their heads up and test the rain.

SCHOMBURGK'S BRICK

Rita Indiana

y thanks for your letter.
nd down the specimens to you.
ere is a good deal of it, the better
one of your people to come here,
ay whether all need come.

Yours truly,

Hercules Read

unreclaimed land, under wood.

SCHOMBURGK'S BRICK

Rita Indiana

Translated by Robin Myers

I
An eminent museum
has made me quite an offer:
to survey days of yore,
or just open its door
with my uncertain science
of ghosts who chat to no one
and dredge up like the waves
the tributary scraps
that slit history's womb,
fasten the donkey's tail

II
This project seeks to hire us
as lettered delegates
atop this shoddy dais
presenting its own thoughts
it wants to stir the nits

inside the snowy wig
and expedite the sword's
smooth ingress to that place
come lithium, come Xanax,
they've nothing on this pain

III

They've gathered in cruel consort
a hemisphere of pens
a ground sloth's skeleton
that creaks and shifts with springs—
low-paid, since budget cuts
"contemptuous of culture"
make night, already dark,
long as a wolfish mouth
the victims of this theft
aren't here for literature

IV

But here I am, declaiming:
I have to pay the rent,
my talent's up for sale
I've sung this song before!
I wish I could respond
with words in Esperanto
but all I have's the language
passed down to me by those
who raped the earth to boast
about it over sandwiches

V

And so a rock's the theme
of my latest commission,
assigned by a curator
duly un-petrified,

for it's an earthen brick
from the Alcázar de Colón
cooked in the blaze of horrors
kindled in Hispaniola
then mixed into formation
with the ground-up teeth of slaves

VI

Schomburgk takes down a letter
describing sights he's seen
and his fervent desire
to congress with his fellows,
all absent on the island;
there's nobody but 'dunces'
contemptible criollos
who've gone and spoiled his stay
despite the august stock
he's brought to the new world

VII

He listlessly recounts
his finds, all paltry bits
of scant vestigial scraps
of 'Indian antiquities',
mini-memorabilia
from legendary sites
established by Columbus,
spots where he ate and drank
the gold there never was,
the blood that's always flowed

VIII

The rock is on display
past the museum doors
the very heart of plunder

clouding the view with gravel
Schomburgk, who claims a piece
hails right from the Alcázar
and plucked this precious scrap
on a royal excursion
into the brutal inland
of a so-called backward nation

IX

Now Don Diego's palace
the Admiral bequeathed him
with showy title deeds
from Columbine disputes
is on the maiden port
that Spain erected in
this region of the Americas,
inaugural outpost
already overcrowded
when Schomburgk disembarked

X

Here's what I'm getting at:
it wasn't Spartan features
that would have been the ticket
to scrounge up remnants there
the palace was some potsherd
jumbled and stacked together
where some of us back then
constructed our own homes
and prostitutes took clients
and colts wandered to graze

XI

It's not hard to imagine
old Schomburgk at his picnic

the streets he ambled down
en route to the Alcázar
a basket full of goodies
a blanket by the cypress
laid out for him to sketch
the landscape and its creatures
the secrets of the fauna
which in this case are cattle

XII

He must have been exhausted
exploring's never easy
the night was growing chilly
and he was celebrating
his latest publication
a portrait of Barbados
cloud-gazing in the grass
when wind blew in and mussed
his blanket, which he caught
and weighed down with a stone

XIII

The clouds are like a spell
they're fickle, treacherous
Schomburgk hastened to pack
and flee the sudden hail
he crouched and gathered up
the fine white linen cloth
the bread and cheese and wine
and crammed them in the basket
held it over his head
and ran the whole way back

XIV

Ensconced at home that night

and sticky with quince paste
his faithful maid Tomasa
discovered half a brick,
'and since the boss is always
inspecting empty vases
and fishes out of water,'
she thought she'd save the rock
and tucked it with a creak
under the mattress pad

XV

The next day, here's what happened:
breakfast didn't appear
and Schomburgk said 'They're gone,
old Miguel and Tomasa!'
the woman was at home
with bags under her eyes
'No one has slept a wink
because of that damned rock
go send it back to hell
which must be where it's from'

XVI

Jumping about with glee
old Schomburgk proudly bayed,
'I do believe I'm blessed,
I owe it all to nature
even the hail complied'
he called for quill and paper
and sealed a formal label
claiming for Queen Victoria
a shred of proto-lore
what say you all? Yes? No?

XVII

This horrifying stone
has traveled time and space
traversing shafts of wind
to make me very nervous
a force, it once was flung
against the stained–glass windows
built with haphazard mirrors
confused by their reflection
a cruel and comic rigging
there must be scores just like it

XVIII
I take it and return it
like in a big-league match
along a path of crumbs
to where? I can't remember
if I can solve this riddle
as it sketches a curve
vast as a mob, it's bound
to fall where it belongs
with heaps of English junk
in some old rummage sale

XIX
And as the ink seeps toward
the end of this attempt
without summoning force
or nattering nonsense
now that the empire's purging
I'll urge a remedy:
don't squash it if it's hard
or churn it if it's wet
don't put it on display
where wounds are festering.

THE MAYA STELE OF PUSILHA

Josefa Sánchez Contreras

THE MAYA STELE OF PUSILHA

Josefa Sánchez Contreras

Translated by Fionn Petch

It was the sowing season when the assemblies commissioned us to accompany a group of English explorers. They had come to our territory looking for buried stones and mounds. At first glance, they looked like the bosses of the mahogany sawmills whose languid bodies formed white patches against the landscape.

The English referred to Belize as British Honduras. To our minds, these lands were called Manche. Among the people who spoke Manche Ch'ol it was well known that the Maya territories we belonged to were split up over colonial and state borders, and were subject to the jurisdictions of Belize, Honduras, Guatemala, El Salvador and Mexico (Yucatán and Chiapas). Despite these artificial distinctions, for a long time we maintained communication with the Zoque, Popoluca, Chinanteco, Zapoteco, Ikoots, Mexica, Garifuna, and many other peoples. In this way, the diversity of our languages was passed on and kept alive the eschatological utopia, that is, the idea that another end of the world was still possible. In this way, since the arrival of the missionaries and the conquistadors, each rebellion and anti-colonial uprising announced the end of one world to give birth to another.

Since the sixteenth century we'd seen countless wars, climate disasters, pilfering and genocides of our peoples. We saw the world ending time and again. By the twentieth century we knew all too well about the discourses erected as scientific that for so long had justified the colonisation of whole territories and peoples. This meant that the arrival of Thomas Athol Joyce and his crew to our lands in 1926 was nothing out of the ordinary. The expedition was funded by the British Museum and was aimed at making a survey of what they called archaeological remains. The group of foreigners comprised Commander James Cooper Clark, a reputed archaeologist with experience in Mexico and Central America; the surveyor Geoffrey Laws, designated by the Royal Geographical Society; the engineer Henry Calverb; Eric Thompson, an anthropologist from Cambridge University specialising in archaeology of the Americas and curator of American antiquities at Chicago's Field Museum; and Mr Hannay, who stood out from the rest for his gift, according to Joyce, of 'managing the native workforce'.

Mr Hannay was, in fact, the first to reach our community. He arrived together with the governor and other colonial officials. It was a fresh spring morning. We were called to the main square and they announced that a group of explorers was recruiting men and women to act as guides and diggers.

Over time, our communities had adopted strategies for receiving outsiders. Their purpose was to protect our territories from colonial incursions. As these were researchers and explorers with supposedly humanist aims, this time the local assemblies delegated to several of us who belonged to the Communal Vigilance Council the task of infiltrating the expedition as local labour. So we signed up to the crew of T. A. Joyce with the aim of keeping tabs on their movements and reporting on the focus of their interests.

Our community debates in those years would rigorously question the colonial character of ethnography and universal history, particularly because they served as a basis for the political discourse promoted by the regimes that oppressed us. That led us to think up a tool to observe those who had constructed these universal narratives in which we were described as indigenous, aboriginal, ethnic groups, and in some cases even as extinct cultures. To understand the gap they had marked between us and them, we began to experiment with a methodology we called *whiteography,* a type of cannibalism that for centuries we had applied to the dominant institutions. So we saw our work keeping watch over the historical territories as an opportunity to use this new tool. We took the group of explorers as our subject of study.

Ten of us, all Manche Ch'ol speakers, were recruited as native labour. It wasn't exactly because of our historical hypotheses, but rather our instinctive knowledge of the deep forest, they said. In the eyes of the explorers, this made us worthy of the status of guides and bearers of food and water.

We tracked the route taken by the outsiders. We soon learned that the crew had set sail from England for the New World on February 2, and reached our coasts on May 3. Once they had landed and recruited our Manche Ch'ol delegation as 'native labour', we plunged into the lush hills of Belize. The explorers tried to navigate the rivers, unsuccessfully. They had conquered the deep waters of the Atlantic, and yet the fresh waters of our rivers proved indomitably rebellious to their oars. In a strange historical continuity, they had to resort to the routes used by the extractive industries: the sawmill roads originally laid out by their forerunners, the merchant colonists.

We walked for days until we reached an ancient site called Lubaantun. It was located in dense forest near the Columbia branch of the Rio Grande. Huge pyramids lost in the undergrowth stood testimony to an extraordinary civilisation. The explorers said that Lubaantun showed unusual architectural features that marked it out from any other Maya site discovered to date. According to their methods, they identified three, perhaps four, architectural periods overlaid in the pyramids. They were a palimpsest of civilisation's relics.

We barely had to turn over the soil to reveal fragments of bowls, jars, incense burners and many other utensils. It was as if long ago a great flood had destroyed and buried that Maya city. Now, we unearthed it like someone digging their own grave. In contrast to our contemporary Maya gaze, archaeologist James Cooper Clark was taking his own inventory: 'painted and moulded Classic-period pottery, jadeite earrings and bones of a possible ruler, a number of early Maya-style pieces suggesting that the buildings buried by later reconstructions belong to a comparatively remote period.'

The anthropologist Eric Thompson was such a devoted follower of Alexander von Humboldt that he had read all his travel diaries, perhaps leading to his desire to know rather than to dominate. We held long conversations together. His eyes shone with the curiosity of a twentieth-century traveller who wanted to get to know the world and its people.

The expedition leader T. A. Joyce, meanwhile, wondered what instruments of war had been used by this enigmatic civilisation. It was perhaps this question that led him to record in detail any tool that might have been a weapon. Obsessively, he fixated on stone fragments and spearheads, flint and obsidian knife blades, polished volcanic rock axes and flint blades with eccentrically shaped flakes. Joyce's fixation was undoubtedly influenced by his involvement in the First World War. He had served as an intelligence officer in the War Office of the General Staff. He even attained the honorary rank of captain.

Our *whiteography* method demanded that we enter the world of this group of explorers. That was how we identified their origin. They came from a society where *Homo economicus* paid tribute in lives to the totem of the war economy. Our observations also suggested that the steps of the monks and scribes of past centuries were followed by those of today's archaeologists, anthropologists and geographers. The former were charged with saving bodies without souls, while the latter were brought here by the desire to rescue the traces of an ancient civilisation they assumed to be extinct.

The rains became storms. The rivers burst their banks and we had to call an end to the expedition. But the unexpected flooding also affected sowing season and we knew difficult times lay ahead when we returned to our communities. Before leaving Lubaantun the group of explorers held an archaeological ritual which consisted of depositing an object from their contemporary culture to let future excavators know they had visited these ruins. Like a metaphor of the passage of the British Crown through our lands, on this occasion they opted to bury a small bag containing a shilling engraved with the effigy of King George the Fifth in the earliest layer of a pyramid.

In their initial excavations the explorers found remains of Maya cities dating from the Classic period, though they suspected there must also be traces of earlier, pre-Classic buildings. One thing struck them as truly extraordinary: the geographical location of the different pyramids formed a broad circle. This finding led them to deduce that at the centre of the circle there must have been a vast metropolitan city-state that ruled over the smaller cities. This was a substantial hypothesis. From then on, the investigations were bent on identifying the state and the empire in ancient Mesoamerican societies. Despite its remoteness from our history as a people and our current conflicts in community life, the hypothesis promulgated by the group of explorers was convincing and even served to feed state nationalism in the early twentieth century. It was soon adopted as a paradigm in some historiographical currents of Mesoamerican Studies and by the Institute of Maya Studies of the National Autonomous University of Mexico.

When Thomas Athol Joyce embarked on the first archaeological explorations of our lands, Belize was still a colony. Almost a century had passed since most Mesoamerican territories had declared their respective independence and formed countries and nation states. By then, the anti-colonial rebellions led by dozens of Maya communities in the sixteenth, seventeenth and eighteenth centuries seemed remote and wholly erased from memory. Also long-forgotten was the fact that the very first independence to be won was that of the black people of Haiti, our Caribbean neighbour. This Afro-descendant uprising took place even before the

French Revolution became the reference point for nineteenth-century criollo liberation movements across the Americas.

The group of English explorers returned to their lands. In fulfilment of our commission to carry out a *whiteography*, the Communal Vigilance Council presented a report to the local assemblies. We emphasised the fact that, in a deliberate act of historical amnesia, archaeology was asking the question: 'Where did the Maya go?' 'Why did a society that was capable of building vast cities collapse?' The hypotheses of anthropologists, archaeologists and historians from the universities of Cambridge and Oxford evoked fierce debates. The self-styled 'collapsist' view argued that the Maya were an empire and their collapse was due to climate change in the sixteenth century, when the demographic debacle in the Americas caused by the Conquest reduced the population to 10% of what it had been. Vast areas of milpa crops and millions of hectares of traditional agriculture had disappeared, leading the natural vegetation to expand at a rapid rate, capturing enormous amounts of CO_2 and generating a planetary cooling known as the 'Little Ice Age'. This phenomenon has been characterised by scholars as the first anthropogenic climate change. From an evolutionary approach, physical anthropology also deduced that in this context the Maya did not survive because they did not know how to nixtamalise the little maize they had. This led to the collapse of an entire civilisation.

The second, 'centrist' viewpoint was based on the results of the first excavations at Lubaantun. The hypothesis was that the Spaniards destroyed the Maya city-state that ruled the territory. Their peoples were left without an overall ruler to ensure the continuity of the lineage. All that remained were the minor cities that had been subordinated to the larger state. These results implied the need for further excavations in the area in order to locate the remains of this Maya metropolis and to solve the riddle of what had happened to the ancient civilisation. Here we drew another parallel. While the travellers of past centuries were looking for El Dorado, now anthropologists, historians and archaeologists were looking for the State.

For this reason, at the 20th Congress of the Royal Geographical Society, scholars argued forcefully for the need to create a Maya Exploration Fund, since early excavations in British Honduras suggested the existence of sites dating to a very early period of American civilisation. They estimated that the annual cost of the expeditions would be around £2,000. To ensure their continuity, the trustees would ask for a capital sum of £40,000 or £50,000 of investment from the public purse. This would provide the resources for extensive exploration of the entire colony over several years.

We learned that amid these discussions, T. A. Joyce secured authorisation from the British Museum for a second exploration. This time his crew was to consist of Captain Edward Louis Gruning and Mr Mark Oliver. The main objective was to probe the upper reaches of the South Stann Creek valley, and to recover an elongated stone carved with numerical inscriptions, letters and figures, which they had named the Pusilha Stele. It was located on the banks of the Moho River. Last spring they had not been able to remove it due to the sudden heavy flooding.

By then, we were living in a period of famine and plague. The previous spring's floods had robbed us of our crops. That's why the assemblies had started a dialogue with the *quilombos* and the Garifuna communities. All of them were tired of the exploitation in the sawmills and in the zafra harvest. Our bodies were being worn away at the same rate as the forest was being felled. In a large regional assembly, the Communal Vigilance Council presented some observations that had emerged from our *whiteography* study: the fragments of utensils we'd dug up were crossing the Atlantic together with thousands of felled trees; the wars were not ceasing but, on the contrary, were continuing in other forms, besieging our territories and, as a result, a great past was being unearthed while paradoxically our lives were being undermined.

The assemblies decided to extend our vigilance committee. For the second expedition of the English we were ten Manche Ch'ol speakers and two Garifunas. For days we walked the route laid out by the sawmills of Mr Pearce, one of the leading colonial traders of mahogany. A landowner showed complicity and generosity to the explorers by lending them ten Caterpillar tractors and two wagons to clear a path through the jungle, as the rivers again proved rebellious.

The first part of the journey was over an open ridge dotted with pine trees. After two hours we entered dense undergrowth. We walked for a long time and with the help of the Caterpillars made our way to some mounds that T. A. Joyce named 'Pearce's ruins', after the mahogany trader. This was a practice typical of the Conquistadors. In the sixteenth century they were already naming rivers after themselves. But it can also be read as a prediction, since for the archaeology of the future Pearce's sawmills will perhaps represent the ruins of a civilisation whose passage through the world will be characterised by an exponential increase in extractive activities on Earth. It will be remembered as a time when humanity destroyed its own habitat.

There's no doubt that the site named 'Pearce's ruins' was substantial. It consisted of a double plaza surrounded by approximately fourteen pyramids and stone platforms. The buildings were buried in undergrowth. They were so entangled in vines that, in many cases, felled trees refused to fall, but remained suspended by creepers entwined in their upper branches. It was absolutely necessary to clear the site in order to distinguish one pyramid from another.

Due to the magnitude of the remains, all of us began to dig. I don't know if it was out of curiosity or because Joyce had ordered it. The fact is that there we were, trying to unearth the traces of what, they said, must have been a great civilisation because of its capacity to build large pyramids. We stayed there for several days. We extracted ceramic artefacts while, muttering in our own language, we wondered what was so extraordinary about these bits of pottery. They were just fragments of items identical to ones we still used on a daily basis. Just as with the metate grinding stones we had dug up at Lubaantun, they were considered worthy of careful recording by drawings and photographs. However, in our communities they were still kitchen tools, part of everyday life. It was like a journey back in time. While we imagined that moment of the flourishing of Maya cities before the Conquest, we witnessed along the way a landscape marked by extractivism: monoculture sugar cane plantations and large deforested areas.

The terrain was hostile to the foreigners. They were plagued by the mosquitoes that bit them relentlessly during the excavation. The rains and storms returned day after day. We were confined to camp on several occasions. These rest days served to further our *whiteography* on the behaviour of the explorers. We included the deductions they had formulated in the course of the day and the questions they directed to the 'native labour'.

Along the way they desecrated tombs. They collected pottery remains which they stored away one by one having recorded them in detail. In the course of the excavations we found fallen steles. All of them were plain, with no inscriptions or anything else that caught the interest of the group of explorers. The objective was to recover the Pusilha Stele, which fascinated them because of its epigraphic inscriptions. To reach the Moho River from the South Stann Creek, we were guided by the map that the surveyor Geoffrey Laws had drawn up during the first exploration. It was a Cartesian map that focused on trade routes and the patches marking timber extraction.

When we reached Pusilha something extraordinary happened: the stele was wrapped in reed mats and sprouting white flowers from amid green ivy. The committee of the Communal Vigilance Council looked at each other in amazement when we realised that the stone the twentieth century explorers were looking for was the same one that the friars of the bishopric of Yucatán, Guatemala, Chiapas and Soconusco had pursued with such zeal in the eighteenth century.

We remembered how in that century the steles had been the object of ecclesiastical paranoia. The bishops accused the indigenous peoples of idolatry. They claimed that they dressed the stones as Virgins and worshipped them heretically. Manuscripts from the Inquisition show that the steles were recorded as speaking stones and redemptive Virgins that evoked the end of the world and incited people to revolt. We decided not to touch it. We communicated with glances that went unnoticed by the explorers. We knew that this scene was repeating itself, and that it was no coincidence. It had been a long time since the steles had last bloomed. What was an omen for our people was a discovery for the explorers.

That second expedition lasted from 12 March to 22 April. Time enough to achieve its twin objectives. The explorers reported: 'the recovery of the largest carved stone from the Pusilha site' and 'the archaeological exploration of an extensive area of the upper part of the South Stann Creek'. They drew maps and plans to which they gave the same names as the rivers of British Honduras.

Believing that they had fulfilled their duty, they set sail for the metropolis once more. They took the new find with them. The Pusilha Stele was exhibited in the halls of the British Museum, along with looted artefacts from many parts of Asia, Africa and the Americas, whose cultures were depicted as exotic in comparison to a mistakenly homogenous humanity.

Meanwhile, we reported again on the whole course of the expedition to our assemblies. They were astonished by the questions the explorers had asked about the supposed collapse of Maya civilisation. In the communities we were well aware that not all the Maya settlements of centuries past had built and governed from great pyramids. Some of us had preferred to strengthen our relationship with the Earth through cultivation. The continued existence of corn cultivation was the most alive and obvious trace of our passage through the world.

The truth is that we Maya hadn't disappeared and the collapse of the vast cities did not mean the extinction of an entire civilisation. Proof of the fact is that the rebellions that in past centuries caused the colonial project to tremble had maintained the long duration of their eschatological and libertarian utopias. Through the dreams passed down from generation to generation by the communities, which had been engraved on the stones and lovingly embroidered and dyed into *huipiles* by the women, they were remembered in the murmurs of the linguistic variants of Mayan transmitted orally by dozens of *tlamemeh*, who continued to travel the trade routes. The *tlamemeh* were porters or bearers who carried cocoa, precious stones, mahogany and cochineal to distant lands.

Our history was quite different from the two hypotheses debated among the specialists in ancient American cultures. After the collapse of the Maya cities, many settlements continued to exist. We will say it again and again: not all Maya inhabited the cities of the great pyramids and not all Maya built a State. On the contrary, there were settlements and ways of life that followed the riverbeds to ensure access to water and to improve the cultivation of the milpa. This way of life created a vast territorial ecosystem. If the state of advancement of cultures were measured by the ability of human settlements to mimic the organic metabolism of the Earth, our peoples would never be considered among the most primitive and savage.

During the colonisation process, our ancestors organised large-scale anti-colonial uprisings to maintain their historical territories. From 1712 to 1743, a rebellious Virgin appeared, announcing the end of the world. It was the same rebellious Virgin that the bishops had refused to recognise in the Church, because they believed that her Castilian robes concealed stelae, talking stones, and stone jaguars. Over the sixteenth century the Spanish had failed to subjugate Yucatán. In 1761 Jacinto Canek led one of the fiercest uprisings, one that shook the Spanish Crown.

All these episodes remained alive in the memory of the people and re-emerged in times of plague and famine. When the colonial condition became unbearable, another end of the world was announced. The steles blossomed and the uprisings of our peoples began.

The reports of our *whiteography* investigations to the assemblies revealed that Thomas Athol Joyce, along with the whole group of explorers, came from an island that in the eighteenth century had built what they called a great industrial civilisation, whose monuments implied the devastation of other worlds. One of the most representative was the steam engine, which relied on an exacerbated demand for mineral and energy resources extracted from all over the planet, including our own territories. This great civilisation was also made possible by the importation of vast quantities of Andean potatoes that saved the northern islands from starvation and fed thousands of labouring bodies that were sacrificed in the coal mines and factories of that extolled Industrial Revolution. It may be that the archaeology of the future will identify this moment as the beginning of the 'capitalocene': the era in which *Homo economicus* strove to make of the Earth one great extractivist mine and set the planet on its course to becoming a plastisphere, in which case surely the archaeology of the future will have to change its tools of archaeometry to plastimetry, enabling it to identify the layers of polypropylene, polyethylene, polystyrene and other plastic derivatives that by then will envelop the Earth. But these are mere assumptions; what we can say for certain is that this century has seen a renewal of the historical process called 'accumulation by colonisation'.

The *whiteography* applied during the years from 1926 to 1930 to the group of explorers was able to confirm that the accumulation of stone objects, steles, ceramics – in short, all the objects that were supposedly employed by the Maya of the past for personal, scientific or artistic uses – was built on the continuity of colonial relations, where each find was implacably turned into a mere thing, and each piece was isolated from its people.

For this reason, the colonial archaeological gaze did not perceive that the 'native labour' was the enigma it really sought to decipher. Those of us who were hired as guides and diggers were part of a contemporary Maya people. Paradoxically, Maya civilisation was treated as one great monolith that eclipsed the vast diversity of languages and communities that we have historically constituted: Tseltal, Tsotzil, Chol, Chontal, Tojolabal, Chuj, Ixil, Mam, K'iche, Achi, Q'eqchi, Cakchiquel, Tzu'uzujil, Sipakapense, Sakapultek, Ch'orti', Poqomam, Itza', Lacandon, Yucatec, Jacaltek, Akatec, Awakatec, Tektitek, Mocho'. There is nothing more anachronistic than identifying pieces dug up as if on a production line and vestiges of colossal cities while failing to notice the people who built them.

It was not long after those days of exploration that the portent heralded by the flowering of the Pusilha Stele came to fruition. In the 1930s, an atmosphere of unrest and discontent spread through the *quilombos* and black villages of the West Indies and Belize. The memory of insurrection, which had been as silent as a dormant volcano, seemed to show signs of a possible eruption. This century had seen the arrival of other political currents that called themselves trade unionist and pro-independence. The word 'independence' began to spread in Belize, and its spread was inevitable. An effervescence of agrarian, identity, indigenous and trade union movements opened a crack in the universal history of the metropolis.

The insurrections were being brought up to date. That is how we came into contact with W. E. B. Du Bois, an activist for the civil rights of black people in the United States. We had a long and endearing correspondence with him about the racism that we, the so-called indigenous and Afro-descendant peoples, experienced in the twentieth century, about the slavery that had made the original capitalist accumulation possible and, above all, about the need to pluralise history and achieve the emancipation that various anti-colonial movements were exercising in those years. The internationalism of the peoples had existed for a long time. It was not the first time that bridges had been built for a common cause between two such distant latitudes.

Later, these conversations influenced Du Bois to question T. A. Joyce's definition of 'black' in the Encyclopaedia Britannica. It was a racist definition that argued the inferiority of the black mentality vis-à-vis that of a white person.

Perhaps it was the prevailing racist approach in the academy that meant the party of explorers didn't realise that the native labour force was part of a Communal Vigilance Council whose function during the years of exploration was to observe and study them. The English group only learned about the *whiteography* when the communities rebelled. At that point, our existence as contemporary peoples became inescapable. In the light of this insurgency, the assemblies decided that we should take our vigilance committee to its logical conclusion. This time it would be transatlantic. It would not be the first time in history that the peoples had gone to the metropolis. As far back as the seventeenth century, delegations of Tlaxcalans had made long journeys to the metropolitan centres to secure titles to their communal lands.

This is what led a delegation of twelve Maya to attend the 25th Congress of the Royal Geographic Society in London. Our speech was entitled: *U kuxtal K-lúumil tían ti u yóol le káajiloób*. When we arrived in those London lands, we were moved to find ourselves in the cradle of Industrial civilisation. We could almost imagine the feeling experienced by James Cooper Clark, Geoffrey Law, Henry Calverb, Eric Thompson, E. L. Gruning, Hannay and Thomas Athol Joyce when they set foot on the great pyramids of what they believed to be a collapsed civilisation. Unlike the group of English explorers, our Communal Vigilance Council did not seek to discover the ruins of their civilisation, but rather to warn that if the process of 'accumulation by colonisation' continues in the twenty-first century, all landscapes will be devastated and another world will no longer be possible.

We developed a sharp critique. The past was not something remote or petrified in colossal stones; in our view, the past lay in the future of the peoples who resisted annihilation. Therefore, it was a question of binding these pieces and these great cities to the living history of the peoples who still existed. Then, the hypotheses of the two currents of colonialist academia – the collapsist and the centrist – began to be questioned. A third position emerged. We upheld it as Maya peoples together with currents of an agrarian archaeology, a libertarian geography, a decolonial historical strand, and a cosmopolitan anthropology.

While our delegation of contemporary Maya visited the showcases of the British Museum, the descendants of the civilisation that carved the Pusilha Stele were rebelling in those historic territories that had long weathered repeated collapse, the world ending over and over. Although in the pale, cold halls of the British Museum the stones did not blossom, we knew that each stele represented a people who resisted dispossession: many still carry the inscriptions of Pusilha in their languages, in their historical memory, and in their persistent defence of their territories.

This story is inspired by the history of the Maya peoples. The name of the speech U kuxtal K-lúumil tían ti u yóol le káajiloób / The heart of our mother earth lives in the spirit of our peoples *was taken from a communiqué of the National Indigenous Congress and the Zapatista Army of National Liberation.*[1] *The names of the explorers and the description of the expeditions were taken from the British Museum archives Eth. 1592, Eth. 513, Eth. 509.* Whiteography – blanquigrafía – *is an anti-racist experiment that anthropologist María Ximena Cortés Flores practises in her writings.*

---

1   http://www.congresonacionalindigena.org/2017/01/03/2a-declara-cion-de-la-comparticion-cni-ezln-sobre-el-despojo-a-nuestros-pueb-los-la-realidad-territorio-zapatista/

THE GLASS ARROWHEAD

Philippe Sands

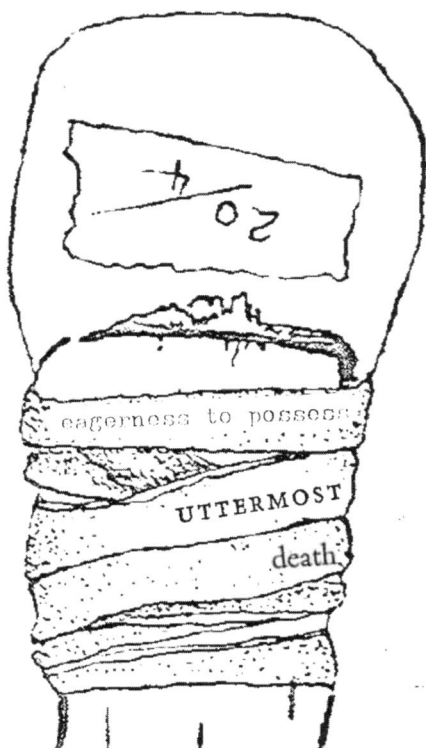

THE GLASS ARROWHEAD

Philippe Sands

It was a quiet summer's evening in November, in Valparaíso, a town of many hills on Chile's Pacific. In a fine old building, in conversation with a publisher, he showed me an old black and white photograph, prompted by a conversation about the Selk'nam, also known as the Ona, an Indigenous community from Tierra del Fuego, in southern Chile. Four men, crouched in the snow, partially clothed in furs, upper bodies exposed to the cold. Faces intent, eyes focused on a distant object. Each poised with a longbow, armed and arrow drawn, an image of symmetry and threat, of power and community.

One archer had a moustache. Looking closely, I noticed a point of detail, highlighted by the dark face of the second archer on the left. It was pale, a speck, no more. A perfectly crafted object, lethal and beautiful. The tip of an arrow. A Selk'nam arrowhead.

★ ★ ★

My interest in the arrowhead was the consequence of a journey many years earlier, to a place called Hagenberg, in central Europe. One thing leads to another. In this small village, in a castle, lived an elderly man called Horst, the son of Otto Wächter, a notorious Nazi Governor and SS leader, and Charlotte, wife and accomplice. Horst, named in honour of the Horst Wessel song, the Nazi anthem, invited me to view his parents' archive, thousands of pages of letters, diaries, notebooks and photographs.

The documents included a letter to his father from an old comrade. Typed in Damascus, Syria, in May 1949, it was sent to Otto Wächter when he resided in the Vigna Pia monastery, on the outskirts of Rome, by a bend in the River Tiber. Hunted for crimes against humanity and genocide, Wächter had taken refuge from pursuers. The writer was Walther Rauff. A former SS officer, a colleague from days in Berlin and Italy, Rauff too was a wanted man, for his role in the gassing of hundreds of thousands of Jews in small vans used as mobile gas chambers. Don't come to Syria, Rauff advised Wächter. Head for South America, a better place of refuge.

Wächter never made it. He expired in grim circumstances in a fifteenth-century Vatican hospital. Walther Rauff, however, made it across the ocean, to Ecuador and a new life as a motor mechanic, then to Chile, in 1958, with wife and sons. They settled in the south, in the city of Punta Arenas, in Patagonia, part of the province of Magallanes. Just across the Straits of Magellan, on the island of Tierra del Fuego, was the smaller town of Porvenir. Rauff divided his time between the two settlements, working as the manager of the *Pesquera Camelio*. He oversaw the packing of the meat of king crabs into small tin cans, for sale around Chile and the world. As tightly as possible, said a young lady who worked for him.

Rauff led a pleasant life, obscure but safe. Then, in the early 1960s, a team of prosecutors from West Germany indicted him for mass murder, for things he had done more than two decades earlier. They sought to extradite him from Chile to face trial in West Germany. The effort failed, for legal reasons of a technical nature – Chile's fifteen-year time limit on the prosecution of such crimes – but it brought a multitude of newspaper articles and much unwanted attention. This did not make him content. Still, life went on in Tierra del Fuego and Patagonia, a notorious man, yet subject to the protective embrace of many in the local community.

★ ★ ★

How could this be, that a local community was able to turn a blind eye to a man with so terrible a past? The question, which hung over my visits, triggered a sense of curiosity about this place where the Rauffs chose to live, at the end of the world. Occasionally I might mention this to an acquaintance. One was a poet with an affinity for the writer Roberto Bolaño, who had invited me to deliver a lecture in Santiago, about the Wächters.

I mentioned my interest in Rauff, a character in my next book. Well known in Chile, he said, 'even taxi drivers talked about him!' He would remind me that Rauff was a character in Bolaño novels, and even made an appearance in Bruce Chatwin's *In Patagonia*. I knew the book, a cult read during university days. It left an impression that lingered but, with the passage of time, the details slipped. In London, I dug up my old copy. The poet was right. Towards the end of the book, Chapter 96, very short, was dedicated to Herr Rauff. 'There is a man in Punta Arenas, dreams pine forests, hums Lieder, wakes each morning, and sees the black strait.' A finely written line, melodic, it opened the imagination.

I read on. Chatwin evoked matters historical, which had also escaped my memory. He met an Englishman, at a palace in Punta Arenas, in a room with a painting of ducks, in which the feet – but only the feet! – were said to have been painted by Pablo Picasso. The Englishman spoke to Chatwin of the Indigenous communities of Tierra del Fuego. A 'pretty low sort', he mused, not like the Incas or Aztecs. 'This business of Indian killing is being a bit overstretched.'

Chatwin wrote also of Dawson Island, across the Strait of Magellan. This was where members of this community, known as the Selknam, or the Ona, once lived, a place to which their descendants still might aspire. Chatwin made a brief visit to the 'black hump', as he called it. It was off-limits in 1975, the era of Augusto Pinochet, and remains so today. He hitched a ride with a local Yugoslav who ran an air taxi. 'I wanted to see the concentration camp where ministers of the Allende regime were held.' He didn't see much, as the soldiers at the airstrip confined him to the small plane.

Dawson was a recent place of brutality. I wanted to know more. When Walther Rauff was around, during the coup d'état of 1973 which brought Augusto Pinochet to power, the island was isolated, inaccessible and largely uninhabited, save for a military base, called Puerto Harris. Yet it was once populated by another Indigenous community, the Kawésqar, or Alacaluf, and also home to the Selk'nam.

The Europeans arrived in the seventeenth century. Spaniards, Germans and British, with culture and ideas. They removed the trees, to create vast sheep farms and make money. The Indigenous communities were not delighted. They objected, caused a nuisance, so the European colonisers decide to remove them too. At the end of the nineteenth century, a local mission of Salesian Fathers, under the guidance of a Monseigneur Fagnano, established a mission on Dawson.

Ostensibly a reserve, where the Indigenous communities could be gathered, the Salesians justified its existence as a place to 'save' aboriginal souls from mass killings perpetrated by European sheep ranchers. Today we would call it an internment camp, a place to hold Selk'nam and others forcibly removed from Tierra del Fuego and Patagonia, to allow more living space for the European colonisers.

I came across another photograph, taken in 1899. It depicted a gathering of members of the Selk'nam and Kaneka Indigenous communities, seated in the grounds of the Colegio de Minas, on Dawson Island. Behind them, in a line, stood men in fine suits and fancy hats. A museum director in Punta Arenas recognised them. Federico Errazuriz Echaurren, lawyer and farmer, also

President of Chile. Rodolfo Stubenrauch, German consul in Punta Arenas, of Prussian origin, a well-respected man of business whose interests extended to sheep farms.

★ ★ ★

This photograph led to another remarkable book, *Uttermost Part of the Earth*. The author, E. Lucas Bridges, the son of Reverend Thomas Bridges, an Anglican missionary, had visited Dawson at the time of the photograph. 'I was on a little steamer which touched at the Silesian Mission,' he recorded, 'where, it was said, about seven hundred Ona were confined.' The women made blankets and knitted garments. The men worked in a saw-mill cutting timber for shipment to Punta Arenas. Bridges had learned their language – his father was the author of a Yahgan/English dictionary, the original of which was deposited at the British Museum, and now resides at the British Library.

There, Bridges conversed with the Selk'nam. They crowded around me, 'splendid specimens', 'decently clad' in discarded or shop-soiled garments, some sizes too small. 'Looking at them, I could not help picturing them standing in their old haunts, proud and painted, armed with bows and arrows and dressed, as of yore, in *goöchilh*, *oli* and *jamni* (head-dress, robe and moccasins)'. There too was a man he called his friend Hektliohlh, who escaped from Ushuaia (today in Argentine Patagonia), was recaptured, then interned on Dawson. He did not complain, but did say that being in captivity made him 'terribly sad'.

'*Shouwe t-maten yaw,*' he said to Bridges. The longing is killing me.

'He did not survive very long,' the author reported. 'Liberty is dear to white men; to untamed wanderers of the wild it is an absolute necessity.'

The sheep farms were profitable, and they brought the European colonisers into conflict with the Indigenous communities. Bows and arrows were pitted against guns, and proved to be no match. The efforts of the Salesian Fathers took the Selk'nam off the lands, to leave them clear for the colonisers. 'I think it's the cheapest way to get rid of them, quicker than shooting them, which is more reprehensible,' a manager of the *Sociedad Explotadora* would say.

As the combination of disease and internment did not achieve what the colonisers desired, they embarked on another way: they hunted the Selk'nam. Bounties were offered, a pound sterling for a pair of ears, creating 'a class of professional head-hunters'. Bridges the son knew one of them as 'Mr. McInch'. It was a pseudonym for the foreman of the *Estancia Primera Argentina*, which was owned by José Menéndez, a businessman of great wealth, born in Asturias, Spain. The foreman's real name was Alexander MacLennan. It was said that he served in

Khartoum with General Kitchener. Chatwin referred to him by his local name, the 'Red Pig'.

MacLennan was said to revel in the killing of the Selk'nam. 'A most humanitarian act, if one had the guts to do it,' he believed, as 'these people could never live their lives alongside the white man.' To hold them in captivity at the Salesian Mission on Dawson was cruel, they would pine away miserably or die from an imported illness, so 'the sooner they were exterminated the better'. By the time MacLennan retired, most of the Selk'nam were gone.

His patron, José Menéndez, wished to express gratitude for years of service. He offered the gift of a gold pocket watch, engraved on both sides. On one side the initials *AMcL*, on the other an inscription written by the master: *Recuerdo de José Menéndez a su buen Colaborador Alex MacLennan* ('Remembrance of José Menéndez to his good collaborator Alex MacLennan').

In time, the people of Punta Arenas expressed their appreciation for José Menéndez. In 1975, during a visit by Bruce Chatwin, they erected a bronze head of José Menéndez in the Plaza de Armas, the main square. 'Bald as a bomb', Chatwin called it. Unaware of the irony, it was alongside a statue of a Selk'nam warrior. Forty years later, protesters removed the bust from its pedestal, painted it green and purple, and placed it by the Selk'nam warrior's foot, with a sign: 'Menéndez Braun, Asesino'.

* * *

MacLennan was not wealthy, but left behind other objects. One was a tie pin, with a triangular feature enclosed in gold: the head of an arrow made of green glass, removed from his body after being launched by a Selk'nam resister. The green arrowhead, which I saw in a photograph, brought me back to another photograph, the one the publisher showed me in Valparaíso.

The bust of Menéndez and the tie-pin prompted me to read more about the treatment of the Selk'nam and other communities from that remarkable part of the world. I learned much.

In 1830, Captain Robert Fitzroy, the commander of *HMS Beagle*, took four young Tierra del Fuegians – of the Yahgan Indigenous community – and brought them to England. The crew gave them names: York Minster, Jemmy Button, Fuegia Basket, and Boat Memory. One died, the three others were returned to Tierra del Fuego on the second voyage of the Beagle, a year later.

The passengers included a naturalist called Charles Darwin. He wrote of a later encounter with Jemmy Button, after the Fuegian was returned to the island. A 'thin haggard savage, with long disordered hair, and naked, except a bit of blanket around his waist', Darwin recorded, who was initially not recognisable as the man who had been deposited 'plump, fat, clean and well dressed'. I do not wish to go back to England, Jemmy Button told them. The change of sentiment, Darwin believed, was most likely caused by the arrival of a 'young and nice-looking wife'. Button brought 'gifts', which included 'spearheads and arrows made with his own hands'. He gave them to Captain Fitzroy.

There were other expeditions to the distant region, some of which returned to Europe laden with objects and people. In Paris, Berlin, London, and elsewhere, the people were made available for public display, in human zoos. In 1881, on the Straits of Magellan, a German sealer kidnapped eleven Kawésqar men, women and children.

Transported to Paris, to be examined by anthropologists, the Jardin Zoologique d'Acclimatation put them on public display. The organisers described them as 'savages – primitive cannibals – of Tierra del Fuego'. After one child died, the group was taken to Berlin, Leipzig, Munich, Stuttgart, Nuremberg and Zurich, for further study. Five more died, those who remained were returned to Punta Arenas.

In 1888, eleven Selk'nam were taken by a Belgian whale hunter, kept in heavy chains, 'like Bengal tigers'. Two died before they could be exhibited at the Exposition Universelle, in Paris, where visitors were entertained by the sight of the captives eating raw horsemeat, to demonstrate their 'voracious cannibalistic instincts'. After Chilean representatives complained to the French Ministry of Foreign Relations, they were taken to London and then Belgium. Moved to jails and workhouses, most died. In 1890, three members of the group were returned to Punta Arenas.

The Europeans were also interested in other objects. Artefacts from Tierra del Fuego were gathered and deposited in museums and places of research, including the British Museum, in London. Somewhere I read that the objects included human remains, and that they were kept, even today, in various locations around London.

I reached out to the Museum, to enquire about the holdings. Curators responded positively, with utmost transparency. They shared papers that summarised what they had on Tierra del Fuego and Patagonia. They gave details of different Indigenous communities – the Yahgan of the Beagle Channel and southern islands, the Selk'nam of the main island of Tierra del Fuego. They provided information about voyages, donations, and donors. They passed on a complete list of holdings, several hundred objects from Tierra del Fuego, gathered by intrepid voyagers I was taught about during childhood. They included Captain James Cook, and sailors and passengers on HMS Beagle. I wondered if the holdings included the 'gifts' offered by Jemmy Button to Captain Fitzroy.

The reported human remains were not among these holdings. It seemed that some from Tierra del Fuego were held at the Royal College of Surgeons – a 'Calvaria, young adult, from Tierra del Fuego' – and the Natural History Museum – a 'thin section cranial' from Ushuaia Bay, Tierra del Fuego, Argentina. The Natural History Museum separated from the British Museum in 1963. Curators at the Human Remains Department confirmed that around thirty items from Tierra del Fuego were held in their collection, including remains from the first voyage of HMS Beagle. Over at the Royal College of Surgeons, a catalogue from 1907 recorded fifteen remains, including the 'skeleton of a female native from Tierra del Fuego' and the 'skull of a male Fuegian… Found in 1879, buried in an old shell-heap near Ushwaia… "a remarkably tall man"… Yahgan'. Today, the only object that remained was a cranium. Who knew what became of the rest. Destroyed in 1941, when London was bombed by the Luftwaffe? Transferred to the Natural History Museum? A visit was restricted to descendants or those engaged in scientific research. Whether this was due to the special sensitivity that attached to human remains, or because information about the circumstances in which they were obtained was problematic, I did not know.

★ ★ ★

The British Museum shared an extensive list of holdings. I identified sixteen objects of interest. Two from Dawson, seven said to be Selk'nam (Ona), and nine identified as Ona or Yahgan. The Museum invited me to visit. As the objects were not on public display, I visited the warehouse near Shoreditch, in the east of London, an innocuous building. It was March and dreary. The objects were brought up from storage, respectfully laid out with care on tables covered in white draping in a room on the first floor. Each had a label, to identify the donor, the source, the date. Many labels were original, from the nineteenth century.

- A bolas, or stone ball, found on the southern extremity of Dawson Island.
- A rush basket, donated on a date unknown.
- A quiver made of the skin of a sea otter, sown with sinew.
- A spear head, made of the bone of a guanaco, a llama-like mammal, donated in the 1920s.
- A harpoon head, made of whale bone.

- A necklace, formed of beads made of bone, in different shades of cream and brown, found on Isla Grande de Tierra del Fuego.
- A necklace made of baby otter teeth, donated in 1870.
- A bow, made of fluted wood and twisted animal fibre cord, sixty-six inches long, acquired by the donor's brother in circumstances unknown. It resembled the one in the photograph with which I began this account.
- The bladder of a seal or a porpoise, filled with red ochre, presented by Lieutenant Thomas Graves RN, in 1855.
- An arrowhead, made of stone, found on Dawson Island.
- A large flat wooden box. It held a collection of arrows, at least eighteen in number, notched and feathered, stored with care, like vintage bottles of wine. As I held them, I noticed that each was unique, different from the last. One amongst them was especially different. The arrowhead, which was bound to the wood with sinew, was made not of stone but of chipped, green glass.

The green stood out, the same green that penetrated the flesh of Alexander MacLennan and brushed his spine. The green that ended up as a tie-pin, embellished with gold.

How curious. What began as a search for one story about a mass killing – by a German, using gas, in a faraway place – led to another. Here in this single object, was a point of connection, one that linked the territory of the Selk'nam to the place that offered refuge to Herr Rauff. For the Selk'nam, as for Rauff, there never was a real accounting. No apology. No reparation.

Here, in a distant warehouse, in one of the world's great museums, out of the public eye, hid a tiny object of resistance. It did not achieve its purpose. It was taken, wrapped, transported, deposited, stored. Now, as it emerged, offering a journey back to another time and place, a memento, a point of connection to a photograph of four men in the snow, hoping to hold off the settlers and their own disappearance.

The bowmen failed. The settlers prevailed. Decades later, their descendants would welcome Herr Rauff to the lands across the Straits of Magellan, and some would even embrace him. Here, the silence was great, the spirit of genocide prevailed, and the sound of impunity was touched by the winds.

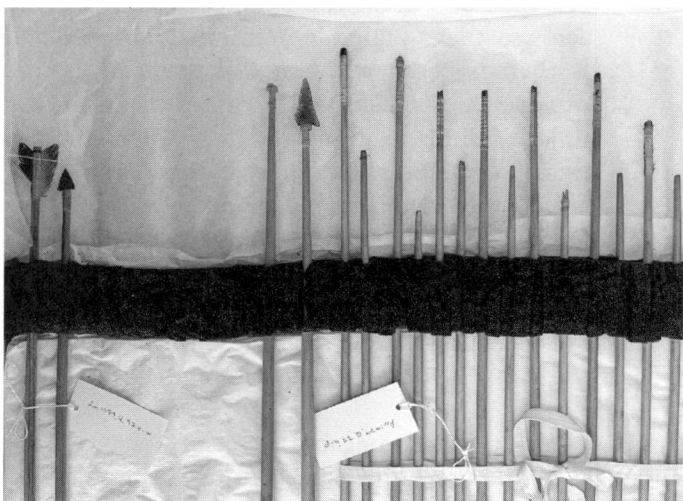

Selected Sources

Books

E. Lucas Bridges, *To the Uttermost Ends of the Earth* (Hodder & Stoughton, 1948).
Anne Chapman, *European Encounters with the Yamana People of Cape Horn, Before and After Darwin* (Cambridge University Press, 2010).
Bruce Chatwin, *In Patagonia* (Jonathan Cape, 1977).
Charles Darwin, *The Voyage of the Beagle* (D. Appleton & Co, 1878).
Elizabeth Dooley, *Streams in the Wasteland: A Portrait of the British in Patagonia* (Rasmussen, 1993).
William Edmundson, *A History of the British Presence in Chile: From Bloody Mary to Charles Darwin and the Decline of British Influence* (Palgrave Macmillan, 2009).
Peter Mason, *The Lives of Images* (2001, Reaktion Books).

Internet

British Museum,
https://www.britishmuseum.org/collection/object/E_Am1957-07-4
The British Presence in Southern Patagonia,
https://rb.gy/3e8asm
Natural History Museum,
https://rb.gy/q5h6yy
Royal College of Surgeons of England,
https://rb.gy/y9t97r

Photo Credits

SELK'NAM GUANACO HUNTERS
Martin Gusinde. Shooting in crouching position. 1918-1924. © Martin Gusinde. Anthropos Institut. Atelier EXB

SELK'NAM IN SCHOOL
'Punta Arenas. Fuegians from María Auxiliadora School (Dawson Island)' in 'Chile Ilustrado', Santiago: Imprenta Barcelona, Year 4, October 1905. Photo by Francisco Bocco de Petris, 1899 © National Library of Chile

SELK'NAM FAMILY
Selk'nam family kidnapped and taken to Paris by Maurice Maitre in 1889. Photo by Adolfo Kwasny, Punta Arenas, Chile. The Museum of World Culture, Sweden (Världskulturmuseet). Public Domain.

SELK'NAM ARROWS
Selk'nam arrows. British Museum collection. Photo by Philippe Sands © Trustees of the British Museum

PAPER IN THE RAIN

Juan Gabriel Vásquez

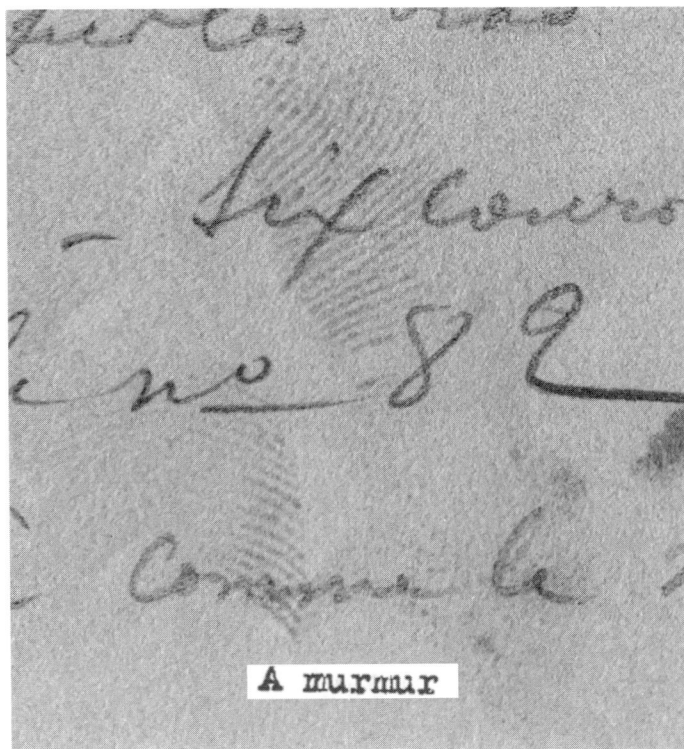

A murmur

PAPER IN THE RAIN

Juan Gabriel Vásquez

Translated by Anne McLean

The message reached me at the end of 2021, during the dead days before the new year, when people leave my suffering city and the streets seem less aggressive, and winds sweep the skies clean and one might get the deceptive impression, in a moment of carelessness, that the world is not a hostile place. The sender was a man I hadn't seen since our student days, in the early nineties. We had both begun law degrees at a central Bogotá university, and were slowly drawn together by our shared dissatisfaction or the worrying revelation that our true vocations lay elsewhere: I had begun to read novels as if my life depended on them, and at some moment I had to surrender to the evidence that writing them, or trying to write them, was all that interested me; for his part, Roberto Giraldo dropped out before the end of the second semester, and over the following years I heard he was living with the Indigenous Tayrona people, that he'd begun to study anthropology, that he'd stopped studying anthropology, that he'd died of yellow fever near Manaus and that he was making a living hunting animals, for white tourists, on the border with Peru. To say that none of these possibilities seemed implausible is perhaps the best description of that unpredictable man; but nothing could have prepared me for him to reappear the way he did, in an email without a subject heading or greeting in which he asked, in the tone of someone who had seen me the previous afternoon, whether the rumour he had heard was true: that I was writing a novel about José Eustasio Rivera.

'If this is true,' Roberto said, 'I want you to meet me at least for a coffee, because I need to ask you some questions. And, unless I'm very much mistaken, what I can offer in exchange is going to interest you.'

His words left me unsettled, to put it mildly. I didn't remember telling anyone about my obsession with writing about Rivera, a figure who had fascinated me for years, and not only due to his extraordinary experiences in the southern jungles where rubber was harvested, or the transformation of those experiences into the beautiful and violent novel *La vorágine* (*The Vortex*) but also due to his premature, mysterious death in an apartment in New York. There were shadowy areas in Rivera's life, spaces where a novel might be able to enter, and I had collected sufficient information about the visible part to be able to start to imagine the invisible parts. But I had already understood by then that we can never completely know the lives of others, the mystery of which is always inexhaustible no matter how publicly they might have lived, and the possibility that Roberto could reveal something useful or new was enough of a lure. So I accepted the invitation from my erstwhile friend, and two days later we met, before noon, at the sunniest table of the Café Pasaje, from which we could see the gates of the university where we first knew each other and, in the middle of the plaza, the statue of the founder of my difficult city, Don Gonzalo Jiménez de Quesada, his bronze head eternally stained with pigeon shit. Roberto barely allowed for two or three pleasantries before lifting a colourful, woven shoulder bag onto his lap, and from the bag he pulled out a copy of *The Vortex*.

'OK, let's get to it,' he said. 'Do you remember the Frenchman?'

Of course I remembered. The man appears halfway through the novel; he's an explorer and a naturalist, according to what Clemente Silva tells the men who listen to his story in the novel, but he's never named; at first it is said that he has come on behalf of a museum or a geographical society, but later it is discovered or believed that the owners of the rubber plantations are paying for his expedition. Clemente Silva is assigned to be his guide, and so he goes, hacking a trail through the jungle with his machete while the monsieur walks along behind with his notebooks and equipment, looking closely at insects and resins, pointing his theodolite at the sky, taking photographs of the trees with a Kodak camera. At some point, the Frenchman begins to understand that the rubber harvesters are not workers, but slaves, and that his hosts are not the cordial, *gracious and honey-tongued* gentlemen who welcomed him so lavishly, but torturers who beat and mutilate and murder the Indigenous workers. Clemente Silva lifts up his shirt, shows the Frenchman his scars and asks whether his back has suffered more than the trees. The shocked Frenchman takes a photo.

From then on, says Clemente Silva, *the photographer's lens documents the workers' bodies*, photographing tortures and wounds and scars *to the enormous displeasure of the overseers*, and the monsieur repeats again and again that these crimes must be exposed, and sends reports to Paris, to London, to Lima. Clemente Silva warns him of the danger he is risking if the owners find out about the photographs and his denunciations, but the monsieur does not back down, and eventually makes the decision to take his complaints directly to the owners. He asks Clemente Silva to convey them himself; Silva obeys, because he cannot refuse. The man who receives him in the company offices is furious with the Frenchman, accusing him of agitating the workers and trying to hobble the business, and rebukes Clemente Silva, pulling up his shirt and vest to compare his back with the one in the photos and stabs his steel-tipped pen into the already lacerated shoulder blade. He orders an overseer to put leg irons around his boots, as punishment, and then, Clemente Silva says, that same overseer marches off with four men, as he says, to take an answer to the monsieur. And that's when we read the sentence that Roberto Giraldo, in the Café Pasaje, recited for me without even looking at the page, with his eyes very wide and his voice somewhat disturbed:

'*The unfortunate Frenchman never emerged.*'

'No, he was never seen again,' I said. 'The jungle swallowed him as well. And what about it?'

'Well, we don't know what happened,' Roberto said. 'No more is said about him in the novel.'

'Because he's a minor character,' I said.

'That's where you're wrong,' Roberto told me. 'Completely mistaken. First: he is important. And second: he's not a character.' He paused and added: 'Let me tell you what I've found out.'

And so he began to tell me about Eugène Robuchon.

He was the eldest son of a photographer from Fontenay-le-Comte, and he could have stayed in his hometown and inherited his father's job and published books of meticulous landscape photos, but he had also grown up reading Jules Verne novels, and one could imagine that something of them had rubbed off on him so that he decided, in 1893, to cross the ocean to the south of the world in search of some relatives who had settled in Montevideo. He lived there for almost three years, learning Spanish and finding out about the strange continent that began when one left the coast, and at a certain moment he started to plan an adventurous trip around Latin America. In February 1896, alone and with no money, armed only with a notebook and a tent, he said goodbye to his relatives in the Plaza de la Independencia and began to walk in the direction of Buenos Aires, with no clear idea of where he was heading and in absolute ignorance of what he would find along the way. He crossed the Andes, passed through Valparaíso, traversed the Atacama Desert at grave risk to his life and finally reached Bolivia, where President Fernández Alonso gave him the rank of second lieutenant and sent him on a mission to set up a customs post on the banks of the Madre de Dios River, which the Bolivian authorities considered the natural border with Peru.

The years that followed turned him into another man. Robuchon paddled every river in the area, cleared the jungle with axe blows, lived with different Indigenous communities and found himself involved in the battles they waged against each other. He was wounded by an arrow and forsaken by his men, and alone and abandoned he learned of the fall of Fernández Alonso. And so he broke his contract and embarked on new explorations on his own behalf and at his own risk; and during one of these he met a young Indigenous woman whose family had been massacred by the Guarayos, and the young woman became his companion and later his partner. According to the documents that Roberto Giraldo discovered, in 1902 the *Daily Telegraph* published the news of the return to France of the explorer with his Indigenous wife, a young woman *of great beauty* who had *fallen to her knees before the white man* and begged him to *save her from her people's enemies*, and also of the baptism and first communion that had been necessary before the marriage. Robuchon and his wife, María Margarita Hortensia Guamiri, lived together in Poitiers for a few months, while he gave talks and made contacts and acquired sponsors to return to the Amazon region, but this time as a real explorer. When he embarked again from the port of Le Havre, Robuchon was no longer the young adventurer who had journeyed through the heart of the South American continent ten years before, but a man with a scientific mission, recognised by the Ministry of Public Instruction and Fine Arts and sent by the Museum of Natural History to collect botanical and zoological specimens from the Madre de Dios basin. He carried a generous provision of books and notepads, a phonograph recorder, a camera, fifty dozen photographic plates and material to reveal them. He wrote detailed letters to the institutions explaining his intention to navigate up the Amazon as far as Iquitos, then up the Urubamba to the Fiscarral pass, make his way overland to Madre de Dios and stay there for two years, collecting geographical and ethnographical documents. Those were his intentions; reality would prove very different.

On 15 June 1903, after a five-week journey, Robuchon and his wife disembark in Manaus. His plan is to leave immediately for Iquitos, but he is prevented by the bureaucracy of customs paperwork and his wife suddenly falling ill. A month will pass before they board the *Preciada* steamer, which covers the route, but the delay does not dampen their spirits: not only do they arrive in a festive city, on the very day Peru celebrates its independence, but on the way Robuchon has met a rich Peruvian businessman, Julio César Arana, who promises help with whatever he might need. But then the setbacks start: Robuchon is the one who falls ill this time, with malaria, and − with both legs and his right arm paralysed − he has to postpone the journey. By the time the paralysis subsides, it is the dry season, and the water level in the rivers he planned to navigate is too low for the boats. At this point Arana, who had spoken to him on board the *Preciada* of his operations in the area, reappears and puts the *Putumayo* steamer, which belongs to his company, at Robuchon's disposal, to take him on a different route up rivers that were still navigable. Robuchon, anxious over the lost time and restless to begin exploring the territories he'd heard so much about, accepts the invitation.

What follows is a five-week adventure that takes Robuchon and his wife up the Amazon to the Putumayo, up the Putumayo to the Igaraparaná and from there to La Chorrera, where Arana's business has one of its most important centres of operation. Robuchon documents everything: the *maringinius*, which are like miniature horseflies, whose bites leave black marks on the skin; the groups of five or six Indigenous men who go out to fish every night, especially if the moon is bright, and return to camp with silurios and palometas and dorados. In Igaraparaná they hear of the rising of the Bora people, who live in the rubber areas of the Cahuinarí, and hear they have killed four white men and eaten them. Work has been suspended until further orders and the workers refuse to return to the forest; Robuchon fears these incidents could disrupt his anthropological explorations.

But he is not daunted: he devotes the following days to walking all over the rubber plantations, in the company of men from Casa Arana, and takes notes and photographs and measures the world as though he were inventing it. He discovers a huge industry that extends over a territory the size of some European countries, shifts unfathomable quantities of money and turns its directors into millionaires. He sees the Murui-Muina men, whom he calls Huitotos, walk through the jungle armed with machetes, slash the tree trunks with precise blows – but only to shoulder-height – and then wait for the sap that flows out to coagulate at the contact with the air, and he finds it hard to believe that the grey paste full of impurities is the rubber on which factories around the world depend.

The figures are impressive: Robuchon hears tell of five hundred thousand kilograms of rubber per year; he is shown graphs and documents; and he transcribes the names of the steamers – the *Liberal* and the *Maizal,* for example – which take the product to the ships whose destinations are New York, Liverpool, Hamburg or Le Havre. He also notes the men of the communities according to the operations centre they serve: on the banks of the Cahuinari the Bora people work; in the centres attached to La Chorrera, the Murui-Muina people. Robuchon lives with them, travels among them, sees their rituals and is terrified and fears them. In a short time he accumulates an immense wealth of material: he annotates everything with scientific precision (*the Huitotos have coppery-brown skin, corresponding to tones 29 and 30 on the chromatic scale of the Paris School of Anthropology*) and records what he can with his camera, from the naked bodies of adolescent girls to the huts and weapons and utensils of daily life. He narrates acts of cannibalism – death by poisoned arrow, dismemberment, the cruel cooking in an earthenware pot – he has survived threats from savages, has touched the cannibals' trophies and has even bought a few, exchanging them for coloured beads. He has seen things few white men have seen.

But maybe he has seen more than he says he's seen.

And maybe he hasn't actually seen what he says he's seen.

And it's here, Roberto Giraldo tells me, where things begin to get complicated.

'All this we know from a manuscript,' Roberto told me. 'That trip ends in October 1903. In August 1904, the Casa Arana persuades the Peruvian government to commission Robuchon to write a report: an ethnographical and anthropological report on the Putumayo zone and its tributaries. The government offers him a good salary and a series of amenities, and puts steamers at his disposal, and assigns him companions. How could he refuse? I imagine as well that he's now feeling like a family man, or feeling that he has the obligations of a family man: because he had found a little Bora girl who was going to be sacrificed by her own people, and decided to buy and adopt her. Anyway: Robuchon signs the contract with the government, and the first thing he does is organise his notes, compile his photographs and write up the story of his explorations, beginning with the distant days of his arrival in Manaus and ending with his return to La Chorrera. He finishes the report, adds the date – 1 October 1904 – signs it with many flourishes and sends it to the Casa Arana. The report is not published, but that does not seem to worry Robuchon. He is focused on other things. He begins to plan a new excursion. It is interesting that he decides to send his wife and daughter to France, as if trying to protect them from something, as if he thought that the places they'd come from were no longer the best places for them. But there's no way to know that for sure.

'Actually, we don't know anything about those months for sure. Robuchon stops communicating with the Paris Geographical Society, but he does write to his father and tells him that he is going to be working for the Peruvian government. He sets up a photography studio in Iquitos, takes portraits of the locals and earns a bit of money doing that. Meanwhile, he carefully prepares for the next expedition. His intention is to leave from La Chorrera, travel up the Igaraparaná River, arrive at the Último Retiro station and return down the Caquetá River: it is a sort of triangle, which covers a good part of the Arana Company's rubber territory. Now then: what was he looking for on that excursion? Was it a scientific mission just like the others? We cannot know, but there are good reasons to think that was not the case. We know he reached La Chorrera in October of 1905, and that he was accompanied by eight Murui-Muinas – two interpreters and six oarsmen – and three employees of the Casa Arana: a Peruvian, a black man from Barbados and an elderly man from Martinique, Félix Cyrille, who spoke French and knew the area well. It seems that a young Murui-Muina woman who was ill with malaria also travelled with them, but I don't know why or what for. The Murui-Muina woman has no name, now she never will: those who have told this story never mentioned her by name... Finally, they were accompanied by Othello, the Great Dane that had been with Robuchon since the beginning of his journeys.

'As soon as they left the problems started. In his haste, Robuchon left the dog behind in La Chorrera, and had to camp at the first stop and send one of the Indigenous men back to retrieve him. The man arrived a day later, with Othello but completely drunk, and Robuchon dismissed him from the mission. They pressed on, up river, making slow progress due to the strength of the current, and spent two nights in one longhouse and one night in another, and on 4 November they finally arrived at Último Retiro. They crossed overland to the River Caquetá and started down it towards the mouth of the Cahuinarí. They were travelling in canoes, and there's the problem: canoes work well when the waters are calm, but there they faced the Angosturas rapids, which are so-named because the course of the river narrows between two high rock walls and there are waterfalls at both sides and the water moves with a force among the rocks capable of overwhelming anyone. It capsized them, of course: the canoe was wrecked in the rapids. They lost what they were carrying, or almost everything they were carrying, but they reached the mouth of the Cahuinarí on a raft, where they were able to set up an improvised camp. There Robuchon, his dog and the ill woman stayed, while the rest went in search of help. It was 3 February 1906.'

'It was the last time Robuchon was seen alive.'

'A rescue mission arrived at the camp ten weeks later, and found it deserted: no trace of Robuchon, no trace of his dog Othello, no trace of the Indigenous woman. The following year Robuchon's manuscript was published, or the Casa Arana had it published by a printer in Lima. It's called *On the Putumayo and its Tributaries*, and it is a fascinating read. For what it says, of course, but also for what it decides not to say. You know better than I do that this is how history is written: not by telling what happened, but making things tell what one wants them to tell. The book has an introduction by Carlos Rey de Castro, Peruvian consul in Manaus and one of Arana's cronies. "Even though painful and unexpected circumstances may have prevented the completion of this work..." That's how it begins, it's priceless. And then it gushes with praise for the Casa Arana, for "the diligent and efficient action of Peruvian industrialists", for the "rational and beneficial exploitation of rubber". He says that the Arana gentlemen, stirred by patriotic interests, have tried to *civilise the Indians*, to bring them a certain amount of culture. That *the Indians* were a *danger for our industry*, but now they are elements of the workforce and wealth creators. And he ends by saying, and this is fascinating, that Señor Robuchon's studies "will have evidentiary force" should it prove necessary to testify to what the Peruvians have done in the area.'

'That's why this book was published at that moment: as proof that the Casa Arana had done no more than patriotically civilise the savages. The Arana Company had not even taken a second glance at the manuscript Robuchon delivered to them three years earlier, and now all of a sudden they publish it urgently and present it as proof. Why? Well, because people had started to find out the truth, Vásquez. Things had started to emerge. That same year of 1907 the Trial of Putumayo began, after two newspapers in Iquitos and one in Lima denounced the atrocities the Casa Arana committed against the Indigenous communities of the area: they wrote of rapes, mutilations, tortures of such cruelty they seemed implausible. But this Señor Rey de Castro, the consul in Manaus, staged an extremely potent propaganda campaign, and the Peruvian government was convinced that the reports were not true: that nothing was going on here. And there are also all the references Robuchon makes to the cannibalistic *Indians*, to the rituals of anthropophagy... Is that true? There are good reasons to doubt it. There was a judge in Iquitos who travelled there to investigate in the middle of the scandal, and returned saying that

Robuchon's report was unfounded: more like a horror novel than a scientific document.'

'And the horror novel served the Casa Arana well. Part of its campaign, of the success of its campaign, was the publication of Robuchon's manuscript, definitive proof that the Indigenous peoples were dangerous savages, and that the Casa was civilising them patriotically by having them work on the rubber plantations. But I have seen the manuscript. I have been in the archives, yes, I have seen the pages Robuchon wrote. I have carefully compared the two things, and sometimes I wish I hadn't. The published book is not the same, Vásquez: there are parts missing. Someone did a very careful edit. Someone edited the truth. You can do that with the truth: you produce a version, a meticulously edited version, and the truth is transformed, becomes something else, is no longer what it was before… Tell me, Vásquez, tell me what we are to make of this passage: "The Huitoto Indian will not agree to participate in the extraction of caucho except very unwillingly." That is not in the published book. Other lines, also about that "Indian": "Keen to recover their independence and the liberty they once had, they believe that the white man, having arrived in their domains in search of the precious tree, will disappear when the tree no longer exists." That is why, Robuchon says, the *Indians* seek the "destruction of the vegetation" which is the cause – listen closely – "of their reduction to slavery".'

'Their *reduction to slavery*: it goes without saying that this is also not in the published book. Yes, Vásquez: I believe Robuchon had begun to realise something, very slowly, the way these things happen. In the manuscript there are these inklings, I don't know what to call them, these little windows through which a version of things is beginning to permeat, a version which is not the one he was given by the men who hired him. And I imagine him handing in the manuscript and then still being concerned, wanting to know more, wanting to find out more… and embarking on new expeditions, or simply leaving his camp to photograph what he shouldn't have photographed. Going to the centres of operation to take photos of the tortured men, the mutilated ones. Doing what the *monsieur* of *The Vortex* does: asking the workers to take off their clothes and show him their scars, and taking photos of all that. The image moves me, why should I deny it: the photographer from the French town, son of a small-town French photographer, the man whose destiny was to take portraits of ladies in enormous hats and gentlemen in livery and bowties and horrible babies in horrible tulle dresses, that photographer, stuck in the Amazon jungle and aiming his camera lens at the destroyed skin of a young Murui-Muina man, at the stump of a mutilated worker. I imagine him taking his final trip accompanied by men of the Casa Arana who have realised what it is that he's doing, but don't tell him. Or maybe he realises that they have realised, but carries on doing it anyway: keeps taking photos, keeps documenting the horror. And he does so thinking nothing's going to happen to him, yes, because everyone knows that nothing ever happens to a white man.'

Roberto Giraldo spoke to me that day – that long day that turned into afternoon and then evening while we talked in the Café Pasaje – of an English captain called Thomas Whiffen, a veteran of the Boer War who in 1908, following in the steps of the legendary Alfred Wallace, arrived in the Colombian jungle and became obsessed with the fate of the disappeared Frenchman. After exploring the area, on his own and without success,

Whiffen met in Iquitos a man from the United States called John Brown, a former worker at the Casa Arana. The man had participated in the mission that failed to find Robuchon after the canoe wreck in the rapids; Whiffen suggested they return to Cahuinarí together, that they look for the location of the last campsite and try to figure out something more about the Frenchman's fate. Later the Englishman related the experience in a book: he described the trip to Cahuinarí, described the arrival at the place where the campsite had been, described the return without answers. He even described an intriguing detail: that he had found a note nailed to a tree, but the paper had been rained on, and there was no way to even begin to guess what had once been written on it. In any case, Captain Whiffen's conclusion was that Robuchon, alone with his dog and the Indigenous woman, had run out of patience waiting for the delayed rescue and had tried to find his own way back, and he was captured or killed by some Indigenous people. His book backed up the Casa Arana's theory.

Then Roberto lowered his voice, as if to avoid anyone at the nearby tables from hearing a secret: as if the story of a Frenchman who disappeared more than a century ago might interest the bored man doing the crossword in *El Espacio*, or the table full of students. And so, in a quiet voice, he told me that John Brown had settled in Puerto Leguízamo after the hellish years of rubber tapping, and there he'd stayed, chewing over his memories and maybe regretting all that he had seen. But in the 1960s, when all the phantoms of the Casa Arana were long gone and nobody even talked about them anymore, he received a visit from some interviewers, maybe anthropologists like Roberto, maybe journalists, maybe just some inquisitive people. He gave them a version that was not the known version. First he told them that the rescue mission had been nothing more than a sham: if they didn't find Robuchon when they arrived at the camp, Brown said, it was because Robuchon was already dead; and if he was already dead, Brown said, it was because he had been taking photographs of the bodies, of the tortures, of the murders. In the second place, the version Captain Whiffen had given in his book – which confirmed the Casa Arana's version of the Frenchman's disappearance – was not true. How did Brown know? Well, because it had been Brown, not Whiffen, who visited the campsite. Brown made the trip, found the place, saw the traces of humans and found the note nailed to the tree, and then he told the captain what he'd seen. And the captain described it all in his book.

I have not seen Roberto since. The novel about José Eustasio Rivera is making slow, somewhat melancholy progress, as if I might not want to reach the end, and every once in a while it gets interrupted by the ghost of the Frenchman, or, to be precise, by the ghost of a piece of paper nailed to a tree trunk. I've spent years thinking about that illegible note, that page that the rain and the sun have damaged irremediably, from which the ink has bled that might once have pointed to Robuchon's whereabouts. Sometimes it occurs to me that the note was not indicating his fate, or even his intentions to leave the camp, but was announcing his death at the hands of a known murderer. Other times I've imagined a brief act of contrition, Robuchon recognising that he should have spoken up before about what he'd seen, or that he should not have written the manuscript that was manipulated by others so it would not say what it was in fact saying. And sometimes I think that the note nailed to the tree and the published book are no different, deep down: they deceive us or lie to us as written history sometimes lies, silencing the truth or twisting it around; they are rinsed papers, ink smudged by the rain that washes everything away, that even washes tears away, or washes away the weeping of others so that we don't have to weep ourselves.

MUMMIFIED WRITER IN THE BRITISH MUSEUM**

Gabriela Wiener

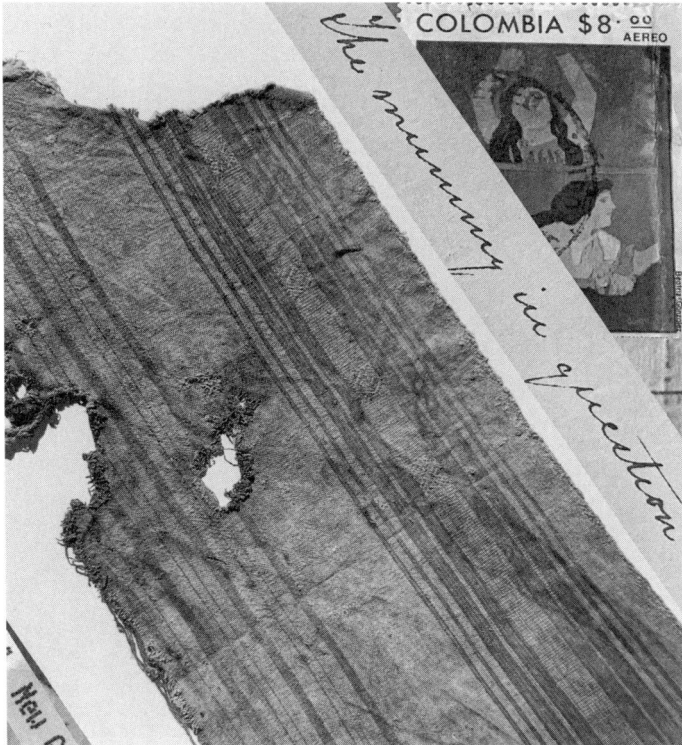

MUMMIFIED WRITER IN THE BRITISH MUSEUM**

Gabriela Wiener

Translated by Frances Riddle

This text is a fictitious correspondence between two authors who knew each other only fictitiously in a fictitious time, after agreeing to work together on a fictitious literary project. The references to the mummies of the British Museum are taken from real letters between researchers and museum employees. The letters between the two authors have been fictionalised through the use of real excerpts from the books of María Emilia Cornejo and Marvel Moreno, which I invite you to seek out and read in their entirety, especially *El tiempo de las amazonas* [The Time of the Amazons] by Moreno and *En la mitad del camino recorrido* [Halfway There] by Cornejo. I have also utilised excerpts from an interview with Moreno and anecdotes that appear in biographic notes on both authors.

I would like to give special thanks to the writer Pedro Casusol for granting me access to his book *Soy la muchacha mala de la historia* (Paracaídas, 2019), a biographical investigation that includes several unpublished poems by

Cornejo; as well as the poet Luna Miguel for her book *El coloquio de las perras* and the references it offered. The last letter from María Emilia Cornejo is composed in reality of four poems in prose from her "French notebook" transcribed first by Casusol. I have also reused at will a letter by Blanca Varela to her friend and poet Reynaldo Jiménez and some extracts from *The Passion According to G.H.* by Clarice Lispector.

Dear Marvel:

How are you? Here I am, in perfect physical and mental condition. They are hopeful that the pills will raise my spirits but, unfortunately, I know, that depends largely on me. I thank you because our project is what gets me out of bed each morning. I've been writing to Penny Bateman for days asking for more information on the Gachancipá mummy but she keeps fobbing me off. I've explained once again that we are writing a text together about those mysterious, long-forgotten remains, mistakenly placed in the department of Egyptian treasures where you saw them for the first time. She doesn't seem to take me seriously as a writer or as a woman interested in the fate of that corpse. Is it because I'm Peruvian? A question that has haunted all Peruvians since time immemorial.

Penny insists that the Gachancipá mummy is male, despite all the evidence we've uncovered. She hasn't been able to tell me whether it's of Peruvian or Colombian origin. And so the wistful bones lie halfway between your shoes and mine. Let's call it dual citizenship. She also doesn't know whether it was donated to the British Museum by Robert Bunch or by that Vélez fellow. I no longer know whether it matters which of the two men laid claim to the discovery. Neither of them truly discovered anything, the mummy would've discovered herself thousands of years ago.

I must confess that ever since I saw that photo I can't stop thinking about those hollow eyes, the way she hugged her knees to her chest as she settled in for death. I think of her as a long lost sister; a pure, exact, unmovable model. Oh, if I had seen her with my own sad eyes like you saw her in the museum, I wouldn't have to only imagine her. Shouldn't it be a crime to shine that spotlight over her head, to keep her locked inside that glass house for all eternity; doesn't it seem like the worst form of neglect? If that's what fame is, I don't want it. I don't want the fame of death.

Sometimes I peer out the window at the sandy hillside I've chosen to call my home and I imagine her as a poor, otherworldly woman emerging from between the huts and children chasing pigeons. Someday I will visit you in Paris, I'm still taking my French lessons, but for now the rooftops of San Juan de Lurigancho fill my landscape.

Today I was unable to get out of bed. I don't want to talk about C. but perhaps I have no choice because I haven't been able to write anything besides this letter. Each day seems like it's secretly, carefully preparing a casual encounter with him on some side street of Lima. You can prepare the unexpected. With C. everything is endless waiting, it's true. I can't stand to look out this window, at this patio that brings back so many memories, the little plant that never flowered. That's the way we were together, we never needed a bed of roses to love each other. And now that he's not here I find warmth in my burial shroud, I curl up like those bones guarding themselves against the brutal cold of the exhibition hall. Time is a butcher, as Blanca Varela would say, and all of a sudden I'm brimming with impatience because we haven't advanced enough with the project, I can't return to what I enjoy most, to the completed poem, to silence, to my life. Maybe it's true that I'm in a hurry to go.

Hugs,
E

Miss Emilia, impatient poet,

How are you? Here I am, doing the opposite of what I should be doing, as always. Disobeying my literary rituals. Disrupting the space allotted for writing. I feel nothing in particular and yet with the tenacity of a small rodent I continue to gnaw at the slice of poisoned cheese, a small existence from which I try to extract I don't know what kind of false lesson, false dream. I don't have much time to write or to think. But my inner lair, that dark, muddy den with its sour, stagnant stench, is battered by storms and shifts in temperature that cause me to commit a thousand lapses, I call Héctor, Gabriel, I call Camila, Piedad. Which is to say that frustration, in certain cases, can challenge or nourish literary work. Failure chafes at inventiveness. If it's not true it's at least a consolation, my friend. I always call my husband 'husband.' And I can't be bothered with that nuisance. But I always think that one of these days something's going to happen and, in some metaphorical inundation, I will sail over my desk, writing, in spite of him, in spite of everything... I hope that by then we'll have some of the answers we're looking for. I'm so bored by those writers who say that answers don't matter, only questions, repeating it over and over until it's stripped of all meaning. And that's the way it is with almost everything. If only I could invent a new language.

I think that men are very unlucky in this world.

They seem to be the winners, but they lose in the end. I've reached an age in which men and women are the same to me. I look at everyone with equal sympathy and antipathy. I like people in general and so I take pity on men. They are so helpless, after all, that I think we should be kind to them, treat them with a bit of compassion. Men do not inspire aggression in me, even in their grand manifestations of machismo, when, like roosters, their crests raise up and turn bright red. It's irritating, like a childish game, albeit a dangerous one.

For now I've cited Varela in this letter, perhaps too many times, but I won't tell you where. Blanca wanted to be a poet, as Octavio Paz called her, poet, in the masculine, as a sign of respect for literature. Not a poetess, never a lady poet, because calling someone a lady poet is akin to calling them a pseudo poet, a lesser poet. Until she had her children. Then she realised she could only write as a lady poet. We are the same text written by a thousand hands. I can't stop thinking about that mummy which you, madam, seem to understand better than me. It must have to do with the amount of time we each spend contemplating the grave. Don't talk to me about C. anymore, if you don't want to.

Kisses,
Marvel

Esteemed Marvel,

You know? No, you don't know. I've only written thirty poems in my life – and I'm referring here to publishable ones – not even enough to fill a book. But I feel that through them I have captured, with as much precision as possible, the colour of my mother's kitchen, the tragically hollow smell of the bed I shared with C. Why do female poets always die, Marvel? I have unfinished pieces about how my body burns with torturous desire in these filthy rooms filled with furtive encounters; I've written about my lovers: sick, drunk poets. About how the ladies on the street make the sign of the cross when they see me pass by. About my guilt and shame. I also wrote about the tautness of the umbilical cord that my twin sister and I shared. If I don't kill myself it's only because it would mean inescapably killing a part of Ana as well. I have only a few more poems than I have years old, Marvel. That's not the case with you. But this mummy of ours has more years than anything else.

What is it that draws us to her? Why do we expect some nameless, purposeless relic to unblock our writing and convert us into a four-armed calligraphic beast? Can you imagine one day being a mummy on display in the museum of women writers? The horror! All the life once contained in our skin, all our love, our abandon, all our intelligence, reduced to dead fuzz on a skeleton, an inert thing to be exhibited, blending into the furniture, falsely arranged back into the position we held when they discovered us to recreate our own marginality. Filed away like relics with a few lines on the wall about what we were, a story invented by someone who got everything about us wrong. Can you imagine being forever underestimated in life, then in death they say that we're the mummy of someone else, some man? That we didn't really write those thirty miserable poems, because we'd be incapable of such a thing, that someone had to have done it for us. And they hide our jewellery and sparkle. Imagine it, because I can't.

Your mummy in her open grave,
Emilia

Dear Emilia,

Now imagine that they sequester our forbidden writings and decide for themselves when and if they can be read, like Sylvia Plath's husband did, making the most compromising pages of her diaries disappear, the ones in which she talked about him, for sure.

To keep from seething any longer I did like you said and wrote back to Penny. She finally answered with some of the information we'd asked for, including several copies of documents, in English and in Spanish, and some photographs. I am enclosing them with this letter. It seems that between the two of us we pestered her enough that she gave in. I told her that we were writing to the museum in our capacity as literary archaeologists. In a way it's true, this is a disinterment.

The mummy in question was presumably found in a cave near Gachancipá, in the canton of Leiva, approximately twenty-nine miles from Bogotá, but that doesn't add up for me. The travellers' letters say she was found by some Indigenous hunters, along with twenty-seven other mummies, but, frightened, they began to destroy them. Can you believe it? Only one was spared. I have given up, as my Aunt Eloísa said, on making sense of the West, where brute force has become a culture that is nothing more than thinly-veiled barbarism. Our lady mummy shares her box with the textiles they found near her, as well as a strange skull. I am convinced that she is a female mummy. I find myself identifying with her more and more. At times your confession about your burning, tormenting bed comes to me like the same blinding light that lit up the sad dimples of my mother, my aunts, my grandmothers, the whole feminine universe of spiritual starvation.

It was perhaps the intensity of life itself that precipitated the death of that woman, in yet another of so many centuries pillaged by men. Don't play their game, Emilia, don't be their perfect victim. Such excessive calculation is inhuman. We know little of the air breathed by that woman, because I do want to think that she is a woman. You know, I was the first woman to enter the College of Economics, and I was crowned queen of the Barranquilla carnival, a role coveted by every girl in that wretched town. Not being named queen is a curse, as you well know. But it is also a trap; there's no escaping. Three books, I've written, which isn't very many either. I may be a wealthy woman but not nearly as affluent as Clarice Lispector, even though we both married diplomats. Perhaps being married to a diplomat is the high price one must pay to dive down deep into existential writing. I'm laughing. Writing is the revenge of the confined.

Another kiss,
Mar

Disquieted and tremulous Mar,

If you're a wealthy woman, I am a miserable wretch. My father was named Amador. But he never seemed to love his extravagant, crazy daughter in constant need of rescue, even though I never felt that way. This explains my early marriage, although C. is the opposite of a diplomat, an absent terror is what he is. I left for love but also to leave. I came to this wasteland populated by the poor or almost poor and Catholic like me, along with many leftists exiled from high society. We believe in God and in the revolution. Basically we are a bunch of stubborn romantics on the outskirts of Lima. I have Susana and Alberto, who are very dear to me. I can count on my neighbours to lend me a cup of sugar or coffee. They will leave soon, I have no doubt, as will I. I believe in the revolution but I am also a woman of flesh and bone, with my desires, my open wounds like live embers. I've never been able to silence my body, a shy voice that rises up loudly at the end of the verse, the way life rises up inside you at the end. It's the only thing I know how to do well: end. These insurgencies go hand in hand. For a real person, love will never be decadent or bourgeois.

But I'm getting off topic, Marvel. We're going to fictionalise that mummy once and for all. Remember my old mummy, Micaela Catari, I call her, made from the poetic and revolutionary and perfect union of Micaela Bastidas and Bartolina Catari, my autochthonous Frankenstein. In that poem, they weren't the wives of any rat-faced men, they were wed to war if anyone. Let's return to our body, comrade. Here, a summary of the documentation that will form the exoskeleton of our text: Cranium, tip of the crown tilted and forehead lowered. Skin still preserved around the cheeks and neck. She once knew how to smile, perhaps out of obligation. The teeth are all missing save one: the mouth is held open with cotton balls. Cotton also are the blankets covering her, painted with a pattern in blue and brown tones showing the image of a face surrounded by rays perhaps representing the sun; she sits with her brilliant bronze-coloured knees raised. I will begin to inspect what's left of the humerus in all its glory, what do you think?

Don't stay away too long,
A kiss from Mrs Cornejo

Emilia,

You remind me of Beatriz, one of the women in my novels. We could say you are the lady with only one tooth. And you are Beatriz. Steadfast in the midst of rebellion. We could say that the still warm and ruined cadaver in the museum was a woman who liked to tell stories, to draw hieroglyphs in the sand or tie knots in rope, who one day said no, but it was too late. Trapped by the toxic and broken logic of the men of her tribe, waiting to be noticed by and receive things from them. Things she undoubtedly wanted for herself. Then she became lost to the labyrinths of her desire and that would be her tragedy, like yours, like mine, like all of ours.

Now I'll say something bold: it was not time that corroded her teeth, they buried her that way, young and toothless, that is my theory. Do you accept it? I believe they killed the woman halfway there, my favourite of your thirty poems, María Emilia, and please stop saying they are too few. There is nothing insufficient about you. You are enough. Take it from this daughter of the Colombian elite. Having a lot taught me to measure the distance between everything and nothing.

We are rewriting the past life of the Marvemilia mummy, let's call her that, a spectre that haunts the lands between Lima and Baranquilla, between the Prado and Pueblo Libre, between up and down, ever constant in her disappearance from the world. I look at her and I imagine she possesses an exaggerated sexuality, painful, like I imagine yours to be, a creature and her desire. She somehow managed to fulfil her desire but she died in the attempt. That is how I will die as well. If power infantilises us, sexuality liberates us, but then it is regulated and punished. They removed the teeth she used to bite through the skin of reality. It is important that history, in this case, should depend on us and not on some cretin like Hemmingway or Lawrence, how I hate him. Did you read *Lady Chatterley's Lover*? What a load of rubbish. They've never been able to write us, why do they keep trying? A woman in love with a penis. Have you ever been in love with a penis? I haven't even been in love with any man, I'm certainly not going to fall in love with a penis. The penis is an abstraction.

Marvel

Dear Marvel,

It's been months since my last letter. And I feel that I've abandoned a body that was already so badly neglected. I have spurned my body anew. And perhaps not only my body. I've abandoned us, Marvel, the mummified woman writer, you, and me. Just one more thing languishing truncated in my life, something that will never come to be. The story is a long one. C. and I were reunited, confident in our love and convinced that it was a good time to become parents. We saw the children of our friends growing up beautiful and strong on the sand pits of Caja de agua, playing *pica pica* at carnivals with colourful balloons. I wanted a love like that for us, vigorous and innocent, that God should help us achieve this, so that one day I could rest my head against his heart. But, dear friend, I lost the baby and then everything began to fall apart between us. C. left the house. And I haven't been able to deal with the insatiable pain of the losses.

Sometimes a little mouse would appear out of nowhere and silently watch me. He would look at me with his body, not his eyes. I would become hysterical every time I saw him because he was not afraid of me. I was afraid of him. One day he stopped coming without even saying goodbye. He simply left, bored by the lack of danger and adventure, I supposed. I searched and searched for him. I must be an awful host, I thought, such an inoffensive human. I no longer have a baby, a husband, or a mouse. One morning I smelled what I thought was a gas leak. I opened a drawer and there was the little mouse, as if asleep, covered in my clothes. Someone had poisoned him. And he chose that place as the placid tomb in which to take his last breath and give me my last fright. Or next to last.

I feel that Marvemilia is all I have left. If we have to speak for anyone it should be for the women who are dead and buried, the bodies hidden away for centuries. Because they cannot speak, their throats choked with the dirt of our ruins. I'm going to speak in the first person because, although it sounds paradoxical, I firmly believe that this is the way we get the most distance from ourselves.

I am the unnamed woman in the cave
She who fornicated with the enemy
And betrayed History
I am the woman
With the deformed cranium
who lost a foetus
from staring at a sunset
until she turned to stone
I am the unnamed woman in the cave

What do you think of my poetic digression? That makes thirty-one poems. Ten more poems than I have years.

Emilia

Ever-present Emilia,

What pain and horror I felt at the summary of your days of silence. I thought of you many times wanting to write and I didn't, I don't know why. Maybe because I was already plagued by bad omens. What to say in the face of so much desolation. How can a miserable slip of paper lined with words provide any consolation for your grief. I no longer know if I'm dead or alive. I am sick. I can't be sure that we are not two ghosts conversing, since we are not here. I don't like to talk about illness, because there's a kind of flirtatiousness in it. To say look at me, I'm sick; it's a manner of seduction, to say pity me. I prefer to suffer in silence.

My Dora, the child of my letters, couldn't go out into the garden without a man from the street touching his phallus. I've put up with plenty as the wife of an important man, the pretty wife of an ugly man. So much condescension. I often see something mouselike in his gaze. When he looked at me I saw life staring back at me. And I didn't see my beauty. If we'd applied Clarice's maxim you would have had to eat that mouse and I would've had to eat my first husband and the second too like cockroaches, antennas, wings, whitish guts and all. To swallow down our fears like communion wafers. To ingest something more alive than we are. I'm afraid of writing, she said, it's too dangerous, everyone who has tried knows this. There is always danger in bringing up what is hidden.

And here I am, a Latin American woman lost in Europe, in exile from exile, without a home, without the tropics, without the Seine, without a breeze, without a tongue, without a boom, without a tomb. That's why I call you *Ever-present Emilia*. Because if not we'll become the forgotten ones. If we take the right path, on the other hand, you can be one of my stories and I can be one of yours and the story of Marvemilia can be both of ours retracing time backwards with our ill-fated logic. We will have many rejections and many lapses, I've got the crazy idea of writing a new novel. Writing is like being locked in a room with a tiger you've caught by the tail. I'm not sure I'll be able to release it, if it will escape, or if I can hold on until the end.

Don't kill yourself yet, Emilia,
Marvel

Dear Penny,
Thank you for your letter and the photocopies. How interesting that you've managed to find what seems to be the original entry. What a shame that it's not clear! Gachancipá, which is around 29 miles from Bogotá, is nowhere near Leiva. Gachantiva, the village near Leiva, is almost 100 miles from there. The cave where those textiles were found was discovered in 1841 whereas Manuel Vélez's cave, by his own account, wasn't uncovered until 1844 or 1845, and that's the cave where he gathered the fragment of blanket donated to the British Museum. Then to top it off, there's the other mummy found by Dawson in a cave near Leiva. Presented by a Mr W. Turner, representative for Her Highness in Colombia. Do you know the date that it arrived to the museum? It is covered in fabric markings. If all those people went to the same cave, and not different caves, what does that mean?

In any case, it's a fascinating puzzle I will continue to attempt to solve. Maybe I should try to visit the Gachantiva cave one of these days. We don't need to continue debating the sex or gender of the mummy in question. I've tired of it. For now I am enclosing a text that Emilia and I wrote about her or about us. We weren't sure what to do with it but I think it might be interesting for the museum to have in its archives. I should also inform you that Emilia died a few months ago.

Best wishes,
Marvel Moreno

Dear Marvel,

I am terribly sorry for the loss of your colleague. She was a kind person and a thorough researcher. I regret that I was not able to aid her more in her work. Thank you very much for the story of the mummy that you sent me, the idea is fascinating and I very much look forward to reading it. I hope you'll soon find a publisher to distribute it to a wider audience.

I am attaching a set of notes made quickly with the little information I have been able to gather on the textiles and Bunch's mummy and an even shorter note regarding what I haven't been able to find on Manuel Vélez's material.

You asked when the mummy donated by M. Turner arrived to the museum: that was in 1838, registered on 11 November of that year. The dates are very close, but unfortunately there is still nothing to connect Turner's material to what Bunch and Vélez discovered, unless Bunch was in Bogotá at the same time as Turner and he wrote to Turner in 1831 about the remains. We still can't know if we're talking about the same person (mummy).

Thank you very much for the text, it will be duly filed in the corresponding archive.

Penny Bateman
Consultant
Museum of Mankind
British Museum, Department of Ethnography
6 Burlington Gardens, London, W1X 2EX

Unforgettable Marvel,

Day after day I've been trying to avoid this task, day after day in which the night, my constant ally, offers refuge to my tired hands. Today, a day of so many words, my hands have stiffened into claws. Where to begin? Impossible to be coherent when so many things are a beginning and an end, when a backwards glance means dizzyingly retracing your steps in an attempt to locate any sign of your trail. Everything ends in every word and every word is a new birth, every word singular and inaccessible created every time I think it. I discover and create worlds – words, words – men, every word begins and ends in the realm of the unimagined.

I begin by saying that nothing happens by mere coincidence, and every word is unique, and everything that happens is unacceptable to the extent that it can happen again or will never happen in the world of things. It's true that a minotaur sleeps under my pillow, and it's true that my house is inhabited by fauns and centaurs, and it's true that every morning I am awoken from dreams by an old hourglass of white sand that burns my hands, true that every afternoon under a tree at the edge of my window I see the waves of my grandparents' blue ocean, true that each night I welcome a man whose face I do not recognise and whose name I can't remember, true that my grandmother's old shoes go for a stroll at dusk, and it's true her rosary prays at night bedside the table in the attic; it's true that in summer the windows speak to the passers-by, and the flowers every day arrange themselves in my mother's old vases, it's true that autumn lends me its leaves so that I may enjoy the soft murmur as they fall, it's true that the river visits us once every two years, leaving behind colourful stones that shine like lamps, blue and brilliant, and it's true that at night in the kitchen they turn into stupid, nocturnal fish; it's true that my grandfather's cousins still cry over his death and it's true that his old cane still takes the dog out for a walk, it's true that the creak of the fourth step on the front stairway knows nothing of visits, nor of the white shirts that my sister irons every day at dawn, it's true that it knows nothing of the violin music played by the poor old man on the corner, the gentle murmur of wind as the carnation falls from his buttonhole and he catches it every time, it's true that the soft wool inside my pillow existed centuries ago in other forms and it's true that not a single head has ever dreamt upon it, it's true that the fork and the chamber pot conspire when we sit at the table and it's true that the coffee we never drink has always been purchased from my uncle, tireless inspector of the native women; our long tradition of dinnertime usurpers is true, and it's true that the silver fades locked away in some mahogany drawer that Aunt Susana dreamed of restoring, it's true that the paintings on the walls talk to my parents and it's true that the termites constantly threaten them, it's true that Cousin Augusta's unfinished collections lie among the jasmines and garden shears, it's true that all the rust in the house gathers together on Friday nights under Aunt Ana's unborn son's windowsill, it's true that the door they bought at the beach travels constantly bringing messages that we never finish answering and it's true that the Thursday train never waits for us more than two hours, and it's true that we travel to the mountains with friends every time a cat dies and a pigeon and it's true that the fields fill with green before our very eyes, and our bare feet at ten o'clock in the morning and the cold headache every night at bedtime, and the kiss we shared a century ago in the door of a café, under the rain, and our hands turned to dust; true is the sun that spies on us as we all dance in winter to the rhythm of some unknown music, and true are the cold faces in the morning at every step along the pavement; true are my shoes that lead me down an unfamiliar path and true is the fear that a mother feels when faced with her child, and true, always, are the things we knew were going to happen published in the morning newspaper, true are the thousand predictions of the gypsy man who responds to each person with their own life, and true is the morning that brings in grapevines and the bras of ruined virgins on a platter, it's true, I know it, that the wife of the old island fisherman stole my cousin's unicorn and it's true that she never forgave her for it.

Every time I feel death abandoning me, tired of so much insisting, every time I feel this inexplicable thing more alive, mixed strangely with a joy for life, I long more than ever for those endless nights of my everyday life. Every time my fears are thrown into relief, age-old fears of the unknown, every time those fleeting moments of happiness come flooding back, I yearn for that self-assured freedom, every time I have to dredge up an odious sentiment before immutable faces, every time my parents' blood poisons my good intentions with its scruples, then I want, I want a thousand different things, to scream on the street, to say please, enough, have a little respect for the person who lives inside me, who you still love, for the inconsolable wanderer who seeks out my destiny. Please, comprehend the incomprehensible.

Because I know that I am here to play the part of the good woman, because I hate without bitterness and sweetly forget that they never loved me, because every day of my life my ribs throb in pain, because my blood is forever poisoned with good intentions, because I defecate and cough, because I feel the pain of every mother's labour, because I am born and die with the rose, because I travel by bus and my shoes hurt, because I aim to solve all problems, because I am as good as the best bread, because I drink from the river as much as I want, because the trees always tell me their names, because I am alone and I am the lonesomeness of night, because the clock strikes ten and I have yet to arrive, because I go to the movies and I smoke, because I come and go from the sea, because everything belongs to me and because I am eternally dispossessed, because I got nothing in exchange for a plate of lentils, because I am and I walk a stone path, because I complain and I suffer, because I don't know how to cry, because I only know how to write, I write!

Goodbye, my dear friend, from mummy to mummy I bid you farewell forever,
Emilia

To Whom It May Concern,

My name is Tim Holden and I am currently employed by the archives office at the British Museum Department of Ethnography. I have not been with the BM long but I am writing because I was surprised to find a text sent to us by a Mrs Marvel Moreno some thirty years ago. It had been filed away in a collection made up of art objects and other vestiges of ancient cultures.

I am aware that Mrs Moreno was a Colombian writer who died shortly after sending us her manuscript. I thought it important to bring the existence of this text to the attention of her descendants because I noticed that the writing in question does not figure in any academic or editorial database. This must mean that it is an unpublished text and probably highly valuable, given the recent resurgence of interest in female Latin American writers who were overlooked for generations. I learned that her novel *El tiempo de las amazonas* was published for the first time only a few years back. Is that correct?

A few weeks ago I began to investigate 'the mummy' referred to so often by Moreno and her co-writer, Peruvian poet María Emilia Cornejo, also deceased, who left an unfinished body of published work. And I have good news. As part of a research project to determine the diet of these populations, I sent a faecal sample from the two mummies to a specialised lab for examination. One of them is clearly male, although its discovery caused much confusion between the museum consultant and the writers. It is a man in a curled position with a large opening in his left ventral, a process used to extract internal organs with the intention of filling them with metals or precious stones.

But the other mummy is that of a woman in a seated position, hairless and with a slight cranial deformation. Which is to say that the theory sustained by Cornejo and Moreno appears to be correct and this mummy was in fact a female from the region around the border between Colombia and Peru, between the Putumayo and Amazon rivers. The origin of the mummy was erroneously entered as Gachantivá, causing the confusion. For at least six centuries, the mummy's people inhabited this region. These discoveries have led us to connect this mummy, who the women called Marvelemilia, with a string of ten perforated seashells, a skein of irregular knots similar to a quipu, and a necklace of three fangs from some fierce animal found nearby. This mummy is also likely related to the mummy of an eleven-year-old girl that was deposited as an offering to this woman, although we cannot confirm whether or not it was her sacrificed daughter. I am happy to remain at your service for anything else you may require. Please direct any further questions to this email address.

Kind regards.

Yours,
Tim Holden

P.S. Many of the objects and documents that made up this collection were destroyed during the war between Colombia and Peru, including some mummies, described as Peruvian. The only older object that could be found referenced in the British Museum archives was the cranium of a deer that seemed to have been confused with the skull of a woman.

AUTHOR BIOGRAPHIES

Selva Almada (Argentina)

Selva Almada is considered one of the most powerful voices of contemporary Argentinian and Latin American literature and one of the most influential feminist intellectuals of the region. Her debut *The Wind that Lays Waste* (Winner of the EIBF First Book Award 2019), was followed by *Dead Girls* (2020), and *Brickmakers* (2021, shortlisted for the Warwick Prize for Women in Translation and the Valle Inclán Prize). *Not a River* (2023, winner of the IILA Prize in Italy) is her fourth book to appear in English. She has also written children's books, a short story collection, and a film diary (written on the set of Lucrecia Martel's film *Zama*). She has been finalist for the Medifé Prize, the Rodolfo Walsh Award and the Tigre Juan Award.

Rita Indiana (Dominican Republic)

Born in Santo Domingo in 1977, lives in Puerto Rico. A key figure in Caribbean literature today, her second novel, *Papi* (2011), became a cult novel as soon as its first lines were published: 'Flowing literature, syncopated reading, street poetry phrasing, amphetamine-fuelled merengue cadence and a strange flavour of beat poetry filtered through magical realism' (Xavi Sancho, *El País*); 'In *Papi* Rita Indiana constructs a narrative edifice with the cadence of merengue and the gaze of a solitary girl that might be a cross between *One Hundred Years of Solitude* and *Misery,* but which ends up as a pop novel insofar as it pays homage to popular culture, both U.S. and Latin American' (Laura Fernández, *El Mundo*). Subsequently, her novels *Nombres y animales* (2013) and above all *La mucama de Omicunlé* (2015, winner of the Caribbean Writers' Association Prize 2017 and translated as *Tentacle*) established her as one of the leading Latin American writers working today.

Josefa Sánchez Contreras (Mexico)

Born in 1991, Josefa Sánchez Contreras is a writer, essayist, researcher and Zoque social activist from the village of San Miguel Chimalapas, in the state of Oaxaca (Mexico). She is a regular contributor to the UNAM magazine and the newspapers *La Jornada* and *The Washington Post*, among others. Her essays have been published by Mexican as well as international universities. In both her research and her literary texts, the themes of her social struggle for territory, Indigenous rights and the gathering of historical information intersect. She is the author of *Camino a Chimalapas* (2016), and co-author of *Cada vez más mokayas: pensares y sentires de zoques contemporáneos* (2022).

Philippe Sands (UK)

Philippe Sands (London, 1960) is professor of law at University College London and a barrister. He has taken part in prominent trials held in the Court of Justice of the European Union, and the International Criminal Court in The Hague, among them the cases of Pinochet, the war in former Yugoslavia, the Rwanda genocide, the invasion of Iraq and Guantánamo. He is author of the essays *Lawless World*, on the illegality of the Iraq War, and *Torture Team,* on the use of torture by the Bush administration. He is a regular contributor to the *Financial Times, The Guardian, The New York Review of Books* and *Vanity Fair,* and appears as a guest on CNN, MSNBC and the BBC World Service. His recent books include *East West Street* (2016), *The Ratline* (2020) and *The Last Colony* (2022). His next book, on Augusto Pinochet and Walther Rauff, will be published in 2025. He expresses deep appreciation to Ashrutha Rai and Monserrat Madariaga Gómez de Cuenca for research assistance, and to Magdalena Araus Sieber of the British Museum for assistance in gaining access to the arrowhead.

Juan Gabriel Vásquez (Colombia)

Juan Gabriel Vásquez (Bogotá, 1973) is the author of two books of stories and six novels: *The Informants, The Secret History of Costaguana, The Sound of Things Falling* (winner of the Alfaguara Prize 2011, Gregor von Rezzori-Città di Firenze Prize 2013 and IMPAC International Dublin Literary Award 2014), *Reputations* (Real Academia Española Prize 2014, Casa de América Latina de Lisboa Prize 2016), *The Shape of the Ruins* (Winner of the Casino da Póvoa Prize and finalist for the International Man Booker Prize) and *Retrospective* (Mario Vargas Llosa Biennial Prize 2022). He has also published two books of literary essays, *El arte de la distorsión* and *Viajes con un mapa en blanco*; a compilation of political articles, *Los desacuerdos de paz*; and a book of poems, *Cuaderno de septiembre*. In 2012 he was awarded the Prix Roger Caillois and he is twice winner of the Simón Bolívar National Journalism Prize. He has translated novels by Joseph Conrad and

Victor Hugo into Spanish. His books have been published in thirty languages.

Gabriela Wiener (Peru)

Gabriela Wiener (Lima, 1975) is a Peruvian writer and journalist living in Madrid. She has published the books *Sexografías, Nueve lunas, Llamada perdida, Dicen de mí* and the book of poetry *Ejercicios para el endurecimiento del espíritu*. Her texts have appeared in both Peruvian and international anthologies and have been translated into English, Portuguese, Polish, French and Italian. She was editor-in-chief of *Marie Claire* in Spain and a columnist for *The New York Times* in Spanish. She won Peru's National Journalism Prize for her investigative reporting on a case of gender-based violence. She is the creator of several performances that she has staged with her family. She recently wrote and starred in the play *Qué locura enamorarme yo de ti*, directed by Mariana de Althaus. Her most recent book is the novel *Huaco Retrato*, translated as *Undiscovered*.

TRANSLATOR BIOGRAPHIES

Anne McLean is a Canadian translator who translates Latin American and Spanish novels, short stories, travelogues, memoirs and other writings by authors including Héctor Abad, Javier Cercas, Julio Cortázar, Gabriel García Márquez and Evelio Rosero. Novels she translated have twice been awarded both the Independent Foreign Fiction Prize and the Premio Valle Inclán. She won the International IMPAC Dublin Literary Award with Juan Gabriel Vásquez for *The Sound of Things Falling* and was shortlisted for the Booker International Prize with the same author for *The Shape of the Ruins*.

Robin Myers is a poet and Spanish-to-English translator. Her translations include *Copy* by Dolores Dorantes, *The Dream of Every Cell* by Maricela Guerrero, *The Book of Explanations* by Tedi López Mills, *Cars on Fire* by Mónica Ramón Ríos, *The Restless Dead* by Cristina Rivera Garza, and other works of poetry and prose. She was a winner of the 2019 Poems in Translation Contest (Words Without Borders/Academy of American Poets). Some of her translations have appeared in the *Kenyon Review*, *The Common*, *Harvard Review*, *Two Lines*, *Asymptote*, *Los Angeles Review of Books*, *The Baffler*, and elsewhere.

Carolina Orloff is a writer, translator and researcher in Latin American literature. In 2016, she co-founded Charco Press where she acts as Publishing Director. She has translated Virginia Woolf into Spanish (*Cuentos Completos*, 2015), and some of her translations into English include *Fate* by Jorge Consiglio (co-translated with Fionn Petch) and Ariana Harwicz's *Die, My Love* (co-translated with Sarah Moses), which was longlisted for the Booker International Prize in 2018.

Fionn Petch is a Scottish-born translator who now lives in Berlin. His translations of Latin American literature have been widely acclaimed. *Fireflies* by Luis Sagasti was shortlisted for the Translators' Association First Translation Award 2018. *The Distance Between Us* by Renato Cisneros received an English PEN Award in 2018. *A Musical Offering*, also by Luis Sagasti, was shortlisted for the Republic of Consciousness Prize 2021 and won the UK Society of Authors Premio Valle Inclán 2021 for best translation from Spanish.

Frances Riddle has translated numerous Spanish-language authors including Isabel Allende, Claudia Piñeiro, Leila Guerriero, and Sara Gallardo. Her translation of *Elena Knows* by Claudia Piñeiro was shortlisted for the International Booker Prize in 2022 and her translation of *Theatre of War* by Andrea Jeftanovic was granted an English PEN Award in 2020. Her work has appeared in journals such as *Granta*, *Electric Literature*, and *The White Review*. She holds a BA in Spanish Language and Literature from Louisiana State University and an MA in Translation Studies from the University of Buenos Aires.

APPENDIX

The following ethnographic documents belonging to the British Museum ('Eth Docs') were shared with the authors and used as inspiration for the stories as well as for each visual composition.

Collages by Diego Atehortúa and Magdalena Araus Sieber, SDCELAR, British Museum.

Selva Almada
Story: Eth Doc 591, Eth Doc 1359, Eth Doc 1415, Eth Doc 1433, Eth Doc 1447
Visual composition: Eth Doc 1433

Rita Indiana
Story: Eth Doc 508, Eth Doc 1344, Eth Doc 1345
Visual composition: Eth Doc 1344, Eth Doc 1345

Josefa Sánchez Contreras
Story: Eth Doc 509, Eth Doc 513, Eth Doc 1592, Eth Doc 1594, Eth Doc 1362, Eth Doc 1369
Visual composition: Eth Doc 509, Eth Doc 1362

Philippe Sands
Story: Eth Doc 1285
Visual composition: Eth Doc 1285

Juan Gabriel Vásquez
Story: Eth Doc 1347, Eth Doc 1424
Visual composition: Eth Doc 1347, Eth Doc 1424

Gabriela Wiener
Story: Eth Doc 456
Visual composition: Eth Doc 456

All documents can be requested via the British Museum website, contacting the Department of Africa, Oceania and the Americas.

© The Trustees of the British Museum

ACKNOWLEDGEMENTS

The editors of this book, Cristina Fuentes, Laura Osorio Sunnucks and Felipe Restrepo Pombo, as well as curators Magdalena Araus Sieber and Diego Atehortúa, are particularly grateful for the help they received from María de las Mercedes Martínez Milantchi (Stanford University), Izara García Rodríguez, Zoe Romero, Iñaki Gabilondo, Chris Bone (Hay Festival), James Hamill, Kate Jarvis and James Dear (British Museum) and Jago Cooper (Sainsbury Centre for Visual Arts). We are also grateful to Silvia Sesé and Lluïsa Matarrodona, editors at Anagrama, and Carolina Orloff, publisher at Charco Press, and editor and coordinator of this English edition

We also want to state that the work carried out at the Santo Domingo Centre (SDCELAR) is possible thanks to the generosity of Alejandro and Charlotte Santo Domingo, and of Don Julio Mario Santo Domingo, in conjunction with Andrés and Lauren Santo Domingo.

CHARCO PRESS

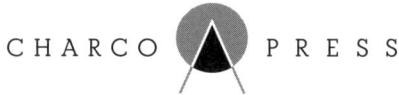

Director & Editor: Carolina Orloff
Director: Samuel McDowell

www.charcopress.com

Explorers, Dreamers and Thieves was published on
80gsm Munken Premium Cream paper.

The text was designed using Bembo 11.5 and ITC Galliard.

Printed in February 2024 by TJ Books
Padstow, Cornwall, PL28 8RW using responsibly
sourced paper and environmentally-friendly adhesive.

FSC
www.fsc.org

MIX
Paper from
responsible sources
FSC® C013056